Broken Hallelujahs

Broken Hallelujahs

Fragments of a Called, Ordained, and Crucified Ministry

Neal J. Anthony

RESOURCE *Publications* · Eugene, Oregon

BROKEN HALLELUJAHS
Fragments of a Called, Ordained, and Crucified Ministry

Copyright © 2025 Neal J. Anthony. All rights reserved. Except for brief quotations in critical publications or reviews, no part of this book may be reproduced in any manner without prior written permission from the publisher. Write: Permissions, Wipf and Stock Publishers, 199 W. 8th Ave., Suite 3, Eugene, OR 97401.

Resource Publications
An Imprint of Wipf and Stock Publishers
199 W. 8th Ave., Suite 3
Eugene, OR 97401

www.wipfandstock.com

PAPERBACK ISBN: 979-8-3852-5310-4
HARDCOVER ISBN: 979-8-3852-5311-1
EBOOK ISBN: 979-8-3852-5312-8

VERSION NUMBER 08/18/25

All scripture quotations are taken from the New Revised Standard Version (NRSV), copyright 1989 © National Council of the Churches in Christ in the United States of America. All rights reserved worldwide.

To my wife, Kim.
With Gratitude

Contents

Acknowledgments | ix
Introduction: Church without High Heels and Make-up | xi

Chapter 1: Crisis Calls: *Upsetting a Chair, Upsetting the Status Quo* | 1
Chapter 2: Visitation: *A Praying Threesome* | 13
Chapter 3: Ministering to Dying and Death: *The Word is Enough* | 23
Chapter 4: Funeral Visitation: *A Casket Crawler* | 32
Chapter 5: Preaching: *Too much goddamn Grace!* | 39
Chapter 6: Ministry Boundaries: *Blinded by our own Goodness* | 48
Chapter 7: Burying Babies: *Shepherding through Death while Celebrating Life* | 60
Chapter 8: Ministering from Grief: *A Special Grief* | 68
Chapter 9: Risking Friendship: *Saying Goodbye while Saying Goodbye* | 74
Chapter 10: Self-care and Ministry: *Just Love your People* | 83
Chapter 11: Church and Politics: *Doing Church in the Time of Trump* | 93
Chapter 12: The Church and Biblical Interpretation: *The Promise of Humor* | 102

Conclusion: Broken Hallelujahs | 115

Bibliography | 121
Subject Index | 123
Scripture Index | 125

Acknowledgments

To my wife, Kim: it was your suggestion that I translate my notes and experiences into a manuscript. You have walked at my side through the peaks and valleys of ordained ministry. You are a parable of God's faithfulness.

To my kids, Owen and Shannon: that you *are* is a gift I can never appreciate enough.

To those who read some version of the manuscript, each at different stages—Ted Bulling, Brian Maas, Jane Armstrong, William Kent Krueger: I am grateful for your comments and suggestions.

To Doug and Jaime: you have been a reminder that, through Jesus Christ, we are priests to one another.

To those whom I have served: I am thankful for our journey together in this "ministry of reconciliation." The crucified and risen Jesus Christ abides on both ends of our shared ministry.

To the staff at Wipf and Stock, especially Matt Wimer and Hannah Starr: I am deeply grateful that this work will see the light of day. And I am deeply grateful that Wipf and Stock is providing that opportunity.

Broken Hallelujahs is not pure theology. Nor is it pure memoir. In many places it comes across as a verbatim, one of those narratives presented in a clinical setting. It is practical theology, yes, but it is more than this. *Broken Hallelujahs*—perhaps—expresses a Word whose communication will not be confined to a single genre or framework.

To all who will read *Broken Hallelujahs*: thank you. May "deep call to deep" (Psalm 42:7) in these pages.

Introduction

Church without High Heels and Make-up

I prefer my wife without high heels. It's not as if when she wears high heels I am disappointed. Certainly not. I enjoy her either way.

My distaste for high heels exists for the sole reason that I can intuit their discomfort. My footwear is chosen for the sake of comfort and function. Style is important, yes. But it is subordinate to practical concerns. My shoes of choice are Clarks Wallabees. Should not my wife—or any woman for that matter—have the same options?

It was reported that Catherine de Medeci was the first woman in European history to don high heels as a fashion statement. It is my understanding that she was short and wanted to appear tall when she was wedded to Henry II of France. Being that her marriage was arranged, she didn't want to be overshadowed by Henry II's much taller mistress, Diane de Poitiers. Mind you, both Catherine and Henry were fourteen years of age. Considering the scenario, I would argue that being vertically challenged was the least of Catherine's issues. It may well be the case that whoever conducted their pre-marriage counseling had to bite their tongue considerably.

It is also my understanding that women wear high heels not just to appear taller, but, more importantly, to give the appearance of longer legs. Longer translates into "slimmer looking." Who doesn't want a pair of slimmer looking legs?

And then there is the matter of make-up. I can't conjure a time in which my wife adorned her feet with high heels without wearing makeup on her face. The use of make-up, as I understand it, can be traced back thousands of years to nearly every culture on the planet. Universally it has been employed—in addition to covering such things as skin blemishes and scars—to enhance feminine beauty.

To the point: the absence of make-up doesn't make my wife less desirable. But make-up does conceal those little things—the freckles, that peculiarly placed mole, those natural lines, those two wrinkles which appear between her eyebrows each time I've frustrated her—that complement who she is. I didn't marry a canvas which has to be redrawn each day. I married the woman with *these* features. The absence of make-up doesn't make her less attractive. It more fully reveals her. Just as she is. It is when she thinks no one is looking, when the make-up is gone, that she most captivates me. *Au naturel.* At the risk of coming off creepy, I think—and perhaps many will agree with me—people are most intriguing when they assume no one is looking in their direction.

In the pages which follow is the church—its ministry—sans high heels and make-up. It is a church with its blemishes and rough edges in full view. This is the church in which and to which I minister each day. This is the church in which I have been ordained to serve Christ's "ministry of reconciliation" (II Cor 5:18).

Nobody can dispute the fact that the Christian church—as expressed in many of her traditions—is famous for her institutional forms, ornately vested assemblies, and moving liturgies through which we encounter the living God revealed in Jesus Christ. But such expressions are *not* the church when she thinks nobody is looking. Such expressions are not the church for 95%+ of the week during even the busiest worship seasons of the liturgical year.

To exclusively envision the church according to such expressions—to keep her in high heels and make-up—I liken to the fantasy of teenage boys I recall from my adolescence: led to believe from their covertly-acquired men's magazines that the ideal woman was airbrushed and perpetually catwalk-ready. For many such a fantasy forever poisoned the prospect of holding a healthy, humanizing image of a woman. Others would come to learn that it is in the beauty of reality, in the beauty of the blemishes, that a woman is more deeply appreciated.

The church in which I have served cannot be contained by such fantasies. The blemishes were present before the vestments were donned and the liturgies were conducted. Only those with such blemishes wear such vestments and officiate such liturgies. All by God's grace.

INTRODUCTION

Perhaps it's due to my personality, or my theology, or a combination of both, but I've always been curious about pastors who assert that their favorite expressions of church revolve around the acts of preaching, Communion, and various other expressions of official assembly. I've often suspected—perhaps unfairly so—that such a focus keeps the fantasy of "church" aloft above the beautiful mess of her people, her relationships, her day-to-day-ness. Shouldn't pastors love their people as much as they love the church's official assemblies and rites?

The only church I know is also the unvarnished church sans high heels and make-up. Long after her rites have been conducted, her assemblies have dispersed, and her vestments have been nicely stowed, the people of Jesus Christ remain the same people they were before such activities had commenced, perhaps—drawing upon a phrase from my tradition—with a renewed "faith active in love."

It is a church whose holiness can only be confessed against appearances. It is this church that I have served for over 25 years as one of its ordained clergypersons. The majority of my time with this lady (my apologies for the sexist metaphor) has been spent without her high heels and make-up on. I am most attracted to her when she thinks nobody is looking.

She—at least according to the tradition of Christianity in which I serve—collectively confesses that she is justified, or made holy, by Christ alone. She is the one to whom Jesus Christ has entrusted the ministry of reconciliation (II Cor 5:18). She is the one through whom, as I write these words, Jesus Christ is renewing the world through his ministry of reconciliation.

But why write such a book, one so revealing of the unvarnished church, in the first place? I am no journaling pietist, that is, one who records their daily spiritual walk with Jesus Christ. Far from it. But this work did begin with a journal. It is one I occasionally visit to record ministerial experiences both positive and negative. It is a journal in which I also occasionally jot down things I have learned and document errors of judgment I have made. The vocation of minister is one of constant growth. It is a vocation which requires the cultivation of a constant, thorough-going self-awareness and self-criticism. Which can be painful. And healing.

Over the course of time the journal's entries have grown exponentially. As time has passed, I have gravitated more and more to the earliest entries. They seem to emanate from another person's experience. Indeed, with the

INTRODUCTION

passing of time, it seems as if many of the experiences I have recorded seem more surreal than when they were originally experienced.

"Did that actually happen?" "Did they actually do that?" "Did I actually experience this stuff?" "Did I actually respond that way?" "Was that the proper response?" "Do pastors really get treated that way?" "Do all pastors share these feelings?" "Do people act that way in all congregations?" "How was I able to serve them while I was experiencing so much pain?" "How was I able to demonstrate love to *that* person?" Better, is the crucified and risen Jesus Christ present amid of all of this?

A ministry, I have come to believe, which is informed and animated by Jesus Christ's ministry of reconciliation will be immersed with the people wherever they are. Which means: such a ministry will be messy. And, at times, it will be painful. The body of Jesus Christ can have sharp elbows and sharper tongues. But those same elbows and tongues may—just the same—facilitate warm embrace and words of grace.

"You need to translate your experiences as a pastor into a book," my wife suggested. She was right. I needed to do so for the sake of reflection and catharsis regarding many of my experiences as an ordained minister. The process of writing has consisted of self-healing and the expansion of self-awareness. But the result is much more than that. There is more here. Such a book as this one, as I came to realize during the process of writing, also has wider purpose and multiple audiences.

For those who are currently serving as ministers this book may well echo similar experiences. Perhaps it may speak to an originally unspoken solidarity of pastoral experience, one we may have been too ashamed of sharing due to its rawness or its litany of judgment errors. Or because we were afraid of revealing the uncharitable and impious feelings and thoughts which have been provoked in us throughout the course of ministry.

Let me be very clear: the church is filled with folks whom ministers both like and dislike. Simultaneously, *like* is an immaterial category of ministry. That is, whether we *like* each other or not, nothing will separate me—the pastor, your pastor—from demonstrating Christ's love *for you*. Pastors are not called to *like* their parishioners. They are called to *love* them. This is the tougher, more authentic calling, one which corresponds to the One who does the calling. Such a *love* permits us to speak and demonstrate truths which *like* will often avoid.

This book will also provide a window into the ministry for prospective clergy *and* lay readers alike. The former will receive a sober, yet

INTRODUCTION

grace-framed taste of Christian ministry. The latter are given—certainly among other things—a sustained glimpse behind the "temple curtain" of ordained ministry. The grace of God dwells on both sides of that curtain.

Ultimately, such a book underscores the reality that high heels and make-up are not only *not* the daily reality of the church, but do not define her beauty. In the words of Martin Luther, "*The love of God does not find, but creates, that which is pleasing to it.*"[1] The love of Jesus Christ makes the beloved beautiful. It is my experience that trouble arises when the church tries to make herself lovely apart from Jesus Christ.

Broken Hallelujahs narrates ministry situations accompanied by reflection upon theological themes which have presented themselves throughout the course of ministry. *Broken Hallelujahs* may even be considered something of an informal *ecclesiology* (in broad terms: "what the church is"). An ecclesiology of this type is, perhaps, a rare species in seminary curricula. Too unofficial. Too raw. Too messy. Too informal. Too many missteps. I have yet to encounter one which captures the glorious messiness, the realness of doing church amid the daily rhythms and patterns beyond official assembly and doctrinal formulation. If, as Luther asserted, the seventh—and final—"mark" of the Christian church is the "holy possession of the sacred cross,"[2] or the identification of the people of God with the cross of Jesus Christ, then before you is an ecclesiology defined by such a "mark."

Such an ecclesiology understands that the bride doesn't need her high heels and make-up on to be considered "church." The One, Holy, Catholic, and Apostolic Church is a creation of the Word of God. Not her attempts at loveliness. Often such attempts are nothing more than wrappings which conceal self-glorifying motives; vice concealed by virtue, so-to-speak. Most of the time *church* refers to the weekly diaspora by which her people are buried without remainder in their service to the needs of community. This diaspora is also known as *vocation*, or serving Jesus Christ precisely where we find ourselves in this blessed, mundane world.

The title of this book, thus its organizing theme, was inspired by the lyrics to Leonard Cohen's *Hallelujah*.[3] Specifically, "broken hallelujah" is

1. LW 31:53

2. LW 41: 164. According to Luther the seven "marks" or holy possessions of the Christian church are Word, Baptism, Lord's Supper, Confession and Forgiveness, the Office of Ministry, Public Worship, and "possession of the sacred cross." See LW 41: 148–166.

3. For a detailing of the journey—from creation to reception to interpretation—which Cohen's *Hallelujah* has made in popular culture, see Light, *The Holy or the Broken*.

a term employed in the third verse of the song.[4] Cohen's *Hallelujah* expresses both a refusal to surrender to despair, and a relentless hope in the face of brokenness. I have come to regard the spectrum of crucified love expressed in the church—through both clergy and laity alike—through the lens of "broken hallelujah." It is a broken hallelujah both concealed by, and radiating within, the cracks of cruciformity, or the shape of Christ's love in this world. It is a broken hallelujah whose shards refract in endless litany the concealed glory of Christ, the countless ways of its giving and receiving. The broken hallelujah—and the new creation it heralds—rises from the depths of human brokenness: broken hearts, broken minds, broken bodies, broken relationships, broken families, broken communities, a broken relationship with God. The aforementioned litany of *brokens* is the soil in which the church's hallelujahs are planted, cultivated, and rise through the Word of God.

It is by no means an asymmetrical praise. It is one which connects clergy and laity. The crucified Christ, his broken hallelujah, abides on both ends of the church's ministry in the broken hallelujahs of his people. Such is the promise lurking in these pages.

+ + + + + + +

This book has been arranged according to various rubrics of ministry, from chaplaincy and visitation to ministering to death and preparing for funerals. Some of the chapters will reflect, in various ways, my experience of ministering from woundedness. The final two chapters focus on—respectively—*doing church* in a politically polarized/tribalized time, and the role of humor in biblical interpretation (which is then applied to *doing church*). The final chapter on biblical interpretation is, perhaps, the most explicitly theological of the chapters.

Each chapter develops a primary ministerial narrative. Yet woven into the development of the primary narrative are other, related experiences. I will not simply narrate ministerial episodes, but—reflective of my journal—present them with the feelings, thoughts, and theological reflection which accompanied them. Some of it will be humorous. Some of it disturbing.

I credit my wife for bringing this song and this book to my attention. In doing so she has provided the perspective and framework for this project.

4. See the epigraph to the book's conclusion—*Broken Hallelujahs*—below for the second half of verse three.

INTRODUCTION

Some of it will be profoundly serious. Some of it raw, coarse. The language, though "rounded off," will reflect this reality. Some of it will reflect mistakes in judgment. All of it expresses my experience as a pastor. We are justified neither by piety nor propriety, but by Jesus Christ alone. We are justified by the faithfulness of Jesus Christ alone.

It has been my desire to communicate—what can be, at times—the realness and rawness of ministry, yet in such a manner that is not repellant. Stated another way: expressing the rawness of ministry is accompanied with a risk, namely, of becoming off-putting. Thus, I have toned down the sharp edges of the real and the raw while attempting to maintain the authenticity of the interactions. Regardless, don't let the form detract you from the content, or the manner by which Jesus Christ's ministry has come to expression.

With the exception of chapter nine, along with references to my own family in other chapters, the personal identities and locations contained within this book have been profoundly masked.

Would you have done things differently, responded differently?

I hope so.

We are not the same people. Your Christ-commitment does not come to expression in the same manner that mine does.

+ + + + + + +

As an old farmer once said to me over a cup of coffee at a country store at the bend of a highway years ago, interrupting himself in the process of lamenting the loss of a portion of his crop to a hailstorm, "You know, pastor, where you can find *sympathy* in the dictionary, don't ya?" A smile migrated across his face. And then he quickly added, "Between shit and syphilis." Together we chuckled. It still makes me laugh. Perhaps it is because experience validates such a sentiment. Yes, kind words are always welcome. And, sadly, they can also be—for the sake of appearing polite—indifference feigning concern. Regardless, whether sympathy is expressed or not, the hailstorm has happened. No amount of sympathy will reverse the circumstances in which one stands.

In the words of that old farmer, this book narrates and reflects upon the experiences of pastoral ministry from the location "between shit and syphilis." Such a phrase is often expressive of the raw—at times seemingly indifferent—contexts from which we call upon the Lord; the locations in which Jesus Christ abides with the people he calls his own. It is where his crazy, unconditional love and life—his glory—is revealed in the concealment of the sinners he has called to participate in his ministry.

It is a messy place. It is a holy place. It's where the Word of God, Jesus Christ, wells up from the depths to lavish in unanticipated ways healing, humanizing, liberating life. It's where the exchange of broken hallelujahs between pastor and parishioner—two sinful, shattered shards on the glorious spectrum of the *imago Dei*—occurs. It is where the crucified Christ—his ministry of reconciliation and healing—dwells, "tents" (John 1:14), on both ends of ministry's acts.

It is my hope that, within the following pages, you will perceive the beauty of the church's crucified praise, the majesty of the broken hallelujah according to a handful of its expressions.

(1)

Crisis Calls

*Upsetting a Chair,
Upsetting the Status Quo*

The ring of the home phone was a bolt of lightning. I felt it deep in my guts. I was jerked into consciousness, yanked into the world of crisis. I glanced up at the red numerals of my digital clock. It was 1:23 a.m. My sleep canopy was shattered into a thousand shards of hard truth about the nature of my vocation.

Those late-night calls serve as sobering reminders. They are reminders that a pastor's time is a rarely a personal possession. Time is shared, communal. It is often the case that they propel one from deep sleep after a long day of ministry—perhaps a full day of home communion and hospital visits, administrative duties, teaching, and evening ministry meetings that have left one drained of vitality—into a context of crisis with little transition time. The anxiety on the other end of the line doesn't consider boundaries. Nor should it. Pastors know this.

Hence, it has become customary for me to conduct a quick ritual of preparation in response to such late-night calls. I might take a quick shower. Certainly, I carve out a bit of time to square myself emotionally through a quick Bible reading followed by prayer. I remind myself out loud three for four times that "I may see some tragic stuff." One doesn't want to spend the first moments of pastoral care in the dead of night at the accident scene—or the suicide scene, or whatever type of scene it is—in shock mode. Such a ritual goes a long way in preparing me for ministry within the context which awaits.

It was 1:23 a.m. With that night shattering ring of the home phone a lightning-quick pastoral calculus was conducted, something like a checklist which took place between the bed and the phone. Let me explain . . .

For the most part, pastors are aware of parishioners whose health is rapidly declining for various reasons. But death is not confined to the realm of predictability. Were it a death at the nursing home, it was my experience that they would contact me in the morning. Were it the death of one of the congregation's elderly folks who resides in their own home, odds were great that it was a widow and I wouldn't be alerted until the next day. At least until mid-morning. She would miss the morning coffee club or quilting group. Then folks would reach out. Perhaps first with a phone call. Eventually someone would enter the home through the back door. Were it the death of an elderly, married man, chances were that he either didn't sleep in the same room as his wife, or he simply slipped away quietly during the night. Either way, the wife would be unaware of his death until the morning. And certainly, it wasn't so-and-so's and so-and-so's families as they were out of town visiting grandchildren.

At the same time, we lived only a handful of blocks from the firehouse (which doubled as an Emergency Medical Station). Nothing was heard. The street from which the emergency vehicles emerged was a shotgun barrel for sirens. This wasn't one of those horrifying situations out on the highway or on the gravel.

My checklist had been exhausted. So why was the phone ringing at 1:23 a.m.? Deal with it. Pick it up. Speak.

+ + + + + + +

"Hello, this is Pastor."

There was a pause.

"Yeah, Pastor, Roy here. We've gotta talk. I need ya to be here quick." The words were spoken with a slight slur. It sounded like the voice of intoxication.

"What's going on, Roy?" I ask.

He replied, the slur becoming more pronounced, "Me and the wife need to, er, sort shit out. Need yer help."

"Crap," I thought to myself, "this may be a tough situation." To what extent, I could only guess. Was this a drunken shouting match? Had it become physical? Was I heading into chaos? I would find out soon enough.

But immediately I had a gut suspicion. Namely, he wanted me to take sides in some type of quarrel. His side. The short back story running through my mind was this: I had only seen him in the church building six times—three Christmas Eve services and three Easter services. He was always friendly. Regardless, *needing* a pastor was a curious matter. Also, I had caught wind of a drinking problem which had created marital turbulence (which by no means made him peculiar in this community). Another initial thought came to me: did his wife finally stand up to him? Did his wife demonstrate an act of self-assertion? Did she dare stand up, push back?

+ + + + + + +

"Who is it?" my wife snapped in her newly awakened state.

"It's Roy," I replied. "I think he's been drinking. And there seems to be some type of marital crisis."

"Unbelievable, it's almost 1:30! I can't believe how disrespectful this is. Can't it wait until the morning?" protested my wife.

I can only imagine what she was thinking at that point in time. Being married to an ordained minister is not always enjoyable. Perhaps she was thinking: "Is this how it's going to be for the rest of our lives? No boundaries? Being "on call" 24-7, 365? With vacation time spent trying to suppress thoughts of the situation(s) to which we'll be returning?" I remember thinking that there needs to be a seminary class which teaches prospective pastors how to "turn it all off" when vacation comes around. Years of experience have provided this wisdom.

"It doesn't sound safe. You're seriously not going are you? Can't it wait until morning?"

I responded, "What if Barb's in a high-risk situation?"

My wife replied, "And if she's at risk, so you'll be at risk."

"I'll figure it out when I get there," I replied. Then I added, "Give me until three to get back. If I'm not back by that time, call the county sheriff. His number's on the cork board in the kitchen. Send him to Roy's. The address is in the directory." I threw on clothes worn the previous day. They were lying at the foot of the bed. I sucked down a cup of instant coffee I had heated in the microwave.

The house was in a larger town up the road. It was approximately ten miles up the black top. On the way there I lowered the windows in my car. The wind whipping through the vehicle not only brought with it a whiff of the nearest hog farm, but created a connection to the world around me which anxiety had choked off.

The thoughts streaming through my head remained undeveloped. The fear of extending them to their logical conclusion made them so. "What if he's in fight-mode? What if she has been knocked around? What if . . .?" Normally a drive up that old black top went quickly. Not on this night. The anticipation of what awaited made the drive seem unending. Within the last mile of town my mind slipped back to a situation which occurred during my chaplaincy experience.

I was a called to a pre-op patient near the end of my shift. A thirteen-year-old, I had been informed, was preparing for a pacemaker replacement. It had been indicated to me that there was "some family tension in the room."

As I approached the hospital room I began to hear their voices. I could hear some "f&*$ yous" and "get the f&*$ out of heres" and "go the f&*$ aways" and a "you're a son of a b*&^%" and a "you're a f&*$%^# a**^%#@." It was a young voice. A girl's voice. I glanced around the corner to see a curtain drawn with the young patient behind it. The mother—a deduction I made based on comments I heard from behind the thin curtain—was at her side. At the foot of her bed was what appeared to be an intoxicated man. It was, I came to learn, her father. He was holding one of California's signature products, an Inn and Out burger. When he wasn't taking bites from it, he was thrusting it toward his daughter in a swaying, drunken rhythm. He taunted her with it.

"Bet you wish you could have what I haaaaaavvvvve." "What a taaaaaaasty burger!" "Toooooooo baaaaad youuuuuuu can't haaaaaaaave one."

"F&*$ you!" the young woman responded. "Go f&*$ yourself!" "You piece of shit!" Get the f&*$ out of here." His young daughter was in a pre-op fast. She was awaiting a procedure that had been pushed back a couple of hours. As I stood there just outside of view, sizing up the situation, I couldn't believe what I was looking at. I couldn't believe what I was hearing.

"Screw it," I thought, "*nice* wasn't going to touch this situation." A benign, pastoral, "fresh-from-seminary-textbook-based-pastoral care approach" wasn't going to make a dent in this situation. Certainly, I could have called for hospital security. But that would have taken time. *Time* continuing under the current circumstances wasn't a blessing for this patient. I commenced a risky pastoral move. It was one that could have made the situation messier.

I made a beeline for the father with the burger at the end of the bed. Eliminate the greatest threat first. That's always been my rule of engagement. I walked up within a few feet of him. "You're outta here. Now."

"What? Who are you? Why? Why do I have to go?" (I wasn't wearing my clerical shirt, just a shirt and tie.)

"I'm not askin'," I replied. "Besides," I added, "you know why."

"What if I don't?"

"You don't have a choice."

"Well, f&*$ you."

Having approached him from his left side, I simply locked arms—my right with his left—and towed him out of the room. I figured this was the only language he would understand. He couldn't have weighed more than a buck seventy-five. He resisted in such a fashion that I was able to feel most of his weight. My clothes paid the price for my proximity to him. I smelled like a smoker for the rest of my shift.

"What the f&*$ are you doing? You can't do this!" he yelled as he was being transported.

"I am," I said. Size and strength can be spiritual gifts, too.

I towed him into the hallway and had a nurse call for security. I went back into the room. His wife was sitting next to the bed. She became still, quiet.

"You're next," I said. "You can either leave on your own, or I can escort you out."

"Okay, okay, I'll go." Slowly she got up, made her way past the curtain. "This is f&*$%^ up and your f&*$%*^# bullshit, I want you to know," she said to me as she made her way past me to the door. I didn't respond. I walked behind her to the door. And then went back in. Only the thirteen-year-old awaiting a pacemaker replacement remained in the room.

As soon as I rounded the curtain which separated the hospital room in half, I was greeted by a very loud, very full-throated, "Who the f&*$ are you?!"

Clearly and calmly, I matter-of-factly replied, "I'm the f&*$^#% chaplain."

Her eyes got big. Her mouth dropped. I made my way to the chair where her mother had been sitting next to her and sat down.

"Chaplains aren't supposed to f&*$^#% talk like that," she insisted.

"But apparently it's perfectly alright for parents to act like that." I responded. I added, "Besides, it's my job to connect with patients where they're at, in language they understand." I paused. And then I added, "It appears I've found a common language, haven't I?"

Though I never saw her again after that occasion, in the thirty or so minutes we were able to connect before her procedure we talked about many things. We talked about boundaries and identities, dreams and empowerment, surviving messed up family systems, not giving in to, not being dictated by, an identity of victimhood and resentment. We talked about how adversity can make us stronger people. We talked about how an identity of victimhood can disempower and destroy us.

It is my hope that, wherever she is, she remembers the "F&*$^#% Chaplain" who humanized her, who *saw* her, who listened to her, who planted a few seeds of empowerment, who witnessed to a God whose liberating presence will not be constrained by the pretense of social decorum. If only for a half-hour in a hospital during pre-op.

I'm there, I've arrived. I pulled into the driveway. I got out of the car. I walked to the front door. I knocked. The door was answered by Barb. Her long, brown hair was disheveled. The make-up which, I'm assuming, she had applied before heading to work the previous morning was now migrating down her face in four or five dark, moist trails. The combination of make-up and tears created a jarring visage.

"Come on in," said Barb, as a contrived half-smile seized her face. It was like so many of those newer, ranch-style houses which dotted the edge of that town. When standing in the front door, the dining room was off to the right. The living room, into which I had entered, gave a view to both the kitchen, to the left, and the bedroom hallway which came off the dining room, to the right. Roy was standing in the kitchen. He wavered like a reed in a stiff breeze. His fire-red hair matched his red face. It was the color of rage and alcoholism.

He greeted me and quickly his face widened to a wild grin. "Pastor, so glad ya came o'er tonight. Sorry got ya outta bed. Needed ya to settle some booolshit."

"Crap," I thought to myself. "He's called me over as an ally."

Barb escorted me to the kitchen table. I sat down. She asked if I wanted a cup of coffee.

"Is some already brewed?" I asked. She nodded. I took a cup. And then a sip. It was lukewarm and old. I remember thinking "beggars aren't choosers." The table was round, about four feet in diameter and covered with a blue and white table cloth. On the table was a mound of canceled checks.

According to Roy, it wasn't the twelve-pack he had consumed in the past few hours. It wasn't the protracted litany of verbal abuse—and who knows what else—which he had dished out. No, the official problem at this hour was that Barb had written checks for such crazy items as milk, bread, some clothes for herself, and a carton of cigarettes. Barb's official problem at this hour was that she had taken the liberty to spend some of her hard-earned money on some basic necessities. To be sure, that carton of cigarettes was an element within the category of *basic necessities.* Adding to Barb's problem at this hour: she appeared to have stood up for herself. She had pushed back.

So, for the first few minutes at the table—Barb on my right, Roy directly across the table—I watched as Roy detailed the canceled checks of the previous month one by one. Each new check he examined was accompanied with "Dumb, f&*$%^# b^%$#." "Wasteful broad." "Selfish c*&^." This verbal barrage created for me what I like to call a *pastoral pause.*

The *pastoral pause*—as I call it—is a short duration of time, perhaps a few minutes, during which, bracketing my emotions to the best of my ability, I simply become an observer. I attempt to discern everything around me from the energy and mood of those in my presence, to the tone of voices, to facial expressions and bodily gestures, to the smell of the room; from the positioning and interactions between the actors, to the clues left strewn around the room, to possible bodily wounds. Are there any firearms in the room? It's an elongated moment in which I simply become an observer with as many of my senses as I can harness. In that pause I was also able to consider a possible course of action based upon what I had observed. All of it was combined with an understanding of the community I had developed over the preceding months and years while serving in it.

It is not uncommon for women who leave husbands in communities like this to be treated with contempt. Unflattering things will be said about Barb for "not making the marriage work." As well, I remember thinking, it might have been the case that she desires to remain in the marriage, satisfied with the trade-off: abuse for stability, drunkenness for social status, no intimacy for financial security. Or, perhaps, *this* was her comfort zone. Perhaps this was the rhythm she trusted, one that was constant and certain.

Perhaps she liked the morning after, the swale of her husband's hangover and his apology-riddled vow to "never do it again" inscribed with the manipulative "I don't deserve you, honey." (Which, in turn, provided a sense of moral authority over her husband.) Maybe that was her currency in this marriage. Perhaps if I made a pastoral move on her behalf, she would turn against me for upsetting the trustworthy status quo. Such is how the bond between victimizer and victim is often maintained.

Though by no means well, I had come know her brothers. Through clues gathered from conversation and the grapevine I had come to learn what they thought of her situation. I sensed they would step up and take her in were the situation to present itself. Had Barb reached this point?

Having watched the tabulation of the canceled checks, having listened to the litany of abuse, having observed the atmosphere, having done a quick social calculus, one thing became clear: I needed to call out the situation and shepherd Barb from it. I emerged from my *pastoral pause* and spoke.

"Roy, you've been verbally abusive. Have you laid a hand on Barb tonight?"

He stopped his tabulating. The litany of slander went silent. He looked up and stared me down. The stare was returned.

"What'd ya f&*$#^' say?"

"Have you laid a hand on your wife?"

"Ya callin' me an abuser?"

"You are verbally. I simply asked if you've laid hands on your wife tonight."

"Ya f&*$#^ takin' her side? This f&*$#^ b%$#@ is spending every last goddamned cent I have. And ya need to see it. That's why I invited [an invitation? really? one I could have turned down?] ya up here. This b^%*# needs to know what she's doin'. Maybe she'll listen for once if yer here. If the pastor's here."

"What I see is a woman who is spending the money she has earned on basic necessities for herself. What I see is a husband who is drunk and abusive. What I see is a woman who is trapped in an abusive, alcoholic marriage with no exit."

"Yer a goddamned lawwww-arrr, Pastor."

I paused.

His words were like a shotgun blast.

I took a breath.

The situation felt as if it had slipped out of my hands; as if it had deteriorated to a point of no return. It was a scenario that still seems unimaginable. The situation felt adrift in waters well beyond any semblance of what was considered adequate boundaries, pastoral or other. Suddenly I felt as if I had been pulled out of the office of pastor. Or pulled more deeply into it.

I became incensed. But it wasn't the kind of anger that escaped self-awareness, as if an untamed beast had burst from a cage. Was I being swept into the electrical current of the hell for which I was seeking to be a ground? Strangely, now in retrospect, I was aware that whatever action came next had profound implications beyond this moment. Whatever followed, I had to own. Whether what came next is right or wrong I still debate. It was a decision, a response, I still hash over in my mind.

Again, I spoke.

"You woke the pastor up at almost 1:30 in the morning to call him a goddamned liar and to take the side of an abuser?"

"Na, na, na, that's not what I'm sayin'. Yer not understannin' me."

I rose to my feet, my chair falling backward. With my left hand I reached for the chair, my fingers cupping its front edge, flinging it onto its back. The clockwise path around the table was covered quickly. I came within a few feet of Roy.

"I've waited for this moment. You woke the pastor up in the middle of the night to call him a liar? Take me on instead of your wife! Threaten me instead! I'm about your size. Let's go."

Had I been swept into the vortex, thus becoming an expression of, the violence I was seeking to diminish as a minister of Jesus Christ? Can one—I have wondered since—harness the ways of the devil in the work of Jesus Christ?

Roy became silent. His face became a wide-eyed stone. He remained in his chair. His face tilted downward. He became a 3-D still life.

Barb—thank God—remained still in those pressurized moments. I'm sure she was stunned. I had lost track of her countenance during my movement toward Roy. Perhaps a pastor provoking her drunken, abusive husband to a challenge in her own home after 2 a.m. was more surreal than everything that had happened until that point.

"No? Not game tonight? Tough guy for your wife but not for your pastor? What a disappointment." I waited for a response. Quiet. The room now had a post-thunderstorm-on-the-plains feel to it.

"You're a bully. Which means you're just a garden variety coward. And this woman next to me? She's not your wife. She's a hostage."

I stood silently over him—my eyes fixed on him—for what seemed like minutes. It was probably only thirty seconds. Maybe twenty. He literally appeared smaller. Barb sat anxiously vigilant. Her eyes were wide. Perhaps waiting for the next wave of aggression which, experience has told her, always rolls in. It didn't.

My eyes scanned the room for where my chair had gone. I had flipped it farther than I thought. With one eye on Roy, I pulled another chair closer to the table at which they were sitting. Nudging it back a little, I again took my seat at the table. Roy sat silently with his eyes fixed on the kitchen floor. Barb, her hands gripping the edge of the kitchen table, sat quietly with a look of disbelief thrown across her face. My gaze was moving back and forth between the couple. The silence was at the level of a shout.

My thoughts swung between "What the hell did I just do?" and "What now?" More than this, how could I get Barb extracted from the situation? Again, I spoke.

"Barb," I said softly, yet sternly, "you're leaving with me." I added, "You can either come with me in my car, or you can take your own car and I'll follow you to where you're going. Either way, you're leaving with me. Your brothers would be more than happy to shelter you. If you remain here you remain at risk. I hope to God you don't return. You don't deserve this abuse."

She silently nodded in agreement. And then I turned my face to Roy.

Upping the volume of my voice I simply said, "Roy, you're a drunk. And you're abusive. You have now arrived where that path leads. I will be having a conversation with the county sheriff about tonight's visit. Keep you on the radar screen, if you know what I mean."

"Pastor," Barb quietly interjected, "I'm going to the back room to get some clothes, some personal items. Give me a couple of minutes. Then we can leave."

"Ok," I replied. My eyes were still fixed on Roy. Roy's remained fixed on the floor.

Roy and I sat in silence for the several minutes it took for her to collect what she needed. Having returned with her possessions, I did something I hadn't previously anticipated doing.

"Barb," I pointed while getting her attention, "I need you to have a seat."

The look on Roy's face was one of "What the hell now?" I reached across the table and grabbed Roy's right hand with my left. I tucked Barb's left hand into my right. And there, at the table, I prayed.

I prayed for Roy's sobriety. I prayed that he would embrace his humanity as a beautiful child created in the image of God. I prayed that he would name his wounds. I prayed that he would name the damage he had inflicted on those around him. I prayed that he would recognize that he was worthy of intimacy and love, as well as being their source.

I prayed that Barb would grow in self-esteem; that she would recognize, as a child created in the image of God, that she was a woman worthy of a man's love, devotion, and intimacy. Not simply his drunken lust. I prayed for Barb's emotional healing. I prayed for her victimhood to become a catalyst for self-empowerment, not dependency and resentment. I prayed for Barb's safety. Together we said *Amen*.

Abusus non tollit is a phrase which appears in Martin Luther's *Large Catechism* regarding the validity of Baptism.[1] Roughly, it means that the misuse of something doesn't nullify its intended purpose/efficacy. Such a logic, I have come to learn, extends beyond sacramental application. It applies to humanity, as well. We are called to seek the image of God in each other no matter how profoundly that image has been distorted. It seems we are in bondage to perfecting ways of warping that image regarding both ourselves and others. Maybe that is what galvanizes my ministry: accompanying folks in perceiving and recovering that image in themselves, in others, in their enemies.

I looked up. Tears were running down Roy's face. Barb's face was awash in resolve. I got up to leave. Barb followed me out. I followed her to a brother's house.

While temporarily living with a brother, a couple of months later Barb filed for divorce. It is my understanding that some of the elders of the community gossiped about the separation and, ultimately, divorce. Some criticized her for not "honoring her marriage vows." Some asserted at the diner that all of it occurred because, well, she was "probably unfaithful" and the Roy "couldn't put up with it anymore." In the destruction of the status quo—often a mask of various forms of captivity—salvation may be stirring. The Christian faith is an exodus faith.

---

1. The complete phrase as it appears in the *Large Catechism* is "*Abusus non tollit, sed confirmat substantiam.*" Translated: "Misuse does not destroy the substance, but confirms its existence." See Luther, "The Large Catechism," 464.

About a year later Roy came to worship. The occasion was his uncle's funeral. Walking through the doors of the church, he was being ridiculed by several of his friends regarding his tie. It was bound together in a sorry-looking knot under his collar. His embarrassment was transitioning to anger.

As the group passed my office, I discreetly motioned for Roy to come into my office. Sheepishly, he moved in my direction with his head down and shoulders collapsed. Once inside my office, he paused. "Come closer," I insisted. We were within inches of each other.

I lifted his collar and loosened his tie. I pulled it over his head. Then, I gently loosed the knot and unfurled the tie. I then placed the tie around my neck and—as I have done with my own son—began to tie it. I then loosened it a bit and pulled it over my head. I slid it back over Roy's head, ultimately placing it around his neck, under his raised shirt collar. I tightened the tie snugly around his neck. Finally, I pulled his shirt collar down over his tie.

Separated by only a handful of inches, his eyes probed mine the entire time. I can't remember a more intimate occasion between myself and a parishioner.

"There, Roy," I said, cupping his cheeks with my hands, "a nice knot. Now you have the best tied tie in the group."

"Thank you, Pastor, you're a good guy."

"And you're a brother in Christ, Roy. There is nothing you can do to change that." I continued, "I spoke truth to you in some direct terms a while back. I care deeply for you. I always have." We embraced. It was a longer hug than I had been accustomed. And snug. He rejoined the group in the sanctuary. The funeral began not long thereafter.

It has always been my goal to proclaim the resurrection promise during a funeral service. It is the promise that the love, the faithfulness, of God overcomes even our deaths. But it is also my experience that the resurrection is adumbrated in an infinite variety of ways before that day of promised new creation.

From a vortex of hell into which we had been swept—thinking back to that night in their home, a night of rage and risk, of challenge and prayer—emerged the slow, first steps of a greater understanding of how the body of Christ is knit together. And the depth of the Love who does so. Seldom do I get the opportunity to demonstrate, to witness, this promise so intimately. It is my experience that the best sermons are often demonstrated beyond the official rites of the church.

(2)

Visitation

A Praying Threesome

Young men often chirp about such matters. It is not uncommon for adolescent boys, shaped by the locker room experiences of life—that realm in which the language of conquest can extend beyond the sphere of competition to encounters with the opposite sex—to carry-on about threesomes. Such arrangements are often a fantasy of adolescent males who have yet to consider sexual expression outside of the realm of objectivity, conquest, and self-gratification.

But, with that said, I have partaken in a threesome of another species. Spontaneous. Unplanned. Unforgettable. Yet, strangely, as I look back, it was a holy, intimate liturgy. One concealed in brokenness, rawness.

It was a routine pastoral home visit. In the morning. At a trailer park on the south side of town. It was my first of several home visits that day, immediately following an early morning nursing home visit. The visit was scheduled for 10 a.m. The drive to the residence, as is customary, was a time of preparation, both mentally (rehearsing names and what I knew about the context) and spiritually. But you need to know . . .

As a dyed-in-the-wool introvert, an INTJ according to the exhaustive version of Myers-Briggs assessment, home visitation for me is the most emotionally and—ultimately—physically taxing aspect of ministry I can think of (ranking right up there with the greeting line following a worship service). But, as one of my colleagues has also said—and I agree—in smaller communities it is ministry's bread and butter. Dare I say: if one expresses a *call* to ordained ministry but balks at the idea of visitation (often consisting of long conversations and home communion) in the homes of 85-year-old widows for a half-hour to an hour at a time, perhaps even two or three times a day, they may not be *called* to ministry within a congregational setting.

It is through home visitation that one comes to learn about the families one is serving. In this setting one learns their stories, the story of the community, its fundamental mythology, its tragedies and triumphs. It is in this setting one comes to understand the priorities and values of the families one is serving and, ultimately, the priorities and values of the community. On a fundamental level of pastoral survival, it is essential that one learns who is related to who.

It is by praying together in the homes of the families one serves that mutual trust is established. In such a context a pastor comes to learn that it isn't merely the *office of pastor*, or the title *reverend*, or the *clerical collar*, or the *academic credentials* that gives them authority, but *trust*. And trust takes time to develop. It is cultivated through listening. And learning stories. And praying together. And laughing together. And crying together. By drinking a cold beer together by the tractor on a warm fall evening after assisting with a long day of work on the farm. By attending an uncle's funeral in another county. By drinking coffee with the quilters.

Ultimately, there is no path to pastoral authority which circumvents the cultivation of relationships and the trust which is their soil. And the surest foundation of such relationships is forged in the homes of a congregation's people. I have concluded that the kitchen table is the One, Holy, Catholic, Apostolic Church's second altar.

The kitchen table is the church's second altar. Just as it was at that elderly couple's home during my first call.

The old man was homebound. The wife, an old Roman Catholic gal who had married into the Lutheran church I was serving, was in worship each Sunday. She was a woman of grace and joy. Her husband, a retired farmer, had become homebound. Once a month we arranged for a visit at their home so that they could enjoy Communion as a couple. After a few months had gone by we invited his Godson and his wife to our gatherings. My wife would come along. Those visits would come close to two hours. Wristwatch time. Fleeting in fellowship time. At their kitchen table we were served cheese and crackers, pickled herring, and cold beer. Jokes were told. Family stories were savored. We cried tears of laughter. We cried tears created by our cognizance of time's passing. Ultimately, we would brush aside the empty beer cans. We would then hold hands in prayer, finally celebrating the Lord's Supper together at that house church altar. Of all the spaces I have considered sacred, that one tops the list. Both the husband and the wife have since died, the wife just recently. I am thankful to have communed at their altar. I am thankful that God erected such an altar in their home.

It was an overcast morning. And a round of home visitation was on the docket for the morning. It was a Thursday.

Having left a nursing home on that same end of town, I was now en route to a trailer park which was adjacent to an industrial tract. The trailer park contained some 40-50 units. The unit to which I was headed contained an elderly couple with a husband who was dying of cancer.

Locating the unit, I pulled up and parked. It was a white single-wide with black faux shutters and a black storm door. Leading up to it was a short walk culminating in a wooden staircase/patio which had been stained red. There was a five-inch gap between the patio and the storm door. The patio wobbled a bit and the red stain was worn, perhaps the result of years of neglected upkeep. The smell of cigarette smoke oozed from the door and windows.

I opened the storm door and tapped on the main door. A voice from just inside answered. It was harsh, gravely. "It's unlocked, c'mon in."

Sitting at the kitchen table—in a hive of cigarette smoke, a pack of cigarettes by her coffee cup—was the wife. Her back was to me. She appeared to have just gotten out of the shower. Her shoulder-length, gray hair was stringy, damp, and combed-back. We'll call her Marge. She was in a thick, yellow, terry-cloth bathrobe.

She made no effort to turn and greet me. I walked around to the opposite side of the table in the cramped kitchen in order to make eye contact. Taking inventory of my surroundings, I looked down. Lo and behold, she was sipping beer from a coffee cup. It was a few minutes after 10 a.m.

"Marge, good morning, I'm the pastor from the church. My secretary called earlier about a visit with your husband, Earl."

"Sum-b*^%# is in there," she replied in a harsh, gravelly voice as she pointed to the bedroom adjacent to the kitchen on the south end of the unit. Her voice appeared to have dropped an octave between inviting me inside and directing me to her husband. There was a slight slur in her words. I was momentarily taken aback.

What did she just say? Perhaps I had not heard that correctly. Did she just call him a "son of b*^%#"? Was that really beer in her coffee cup? Could she be intoxicated this early in the day? Let's be clear on this matter though: if inebriation is common in this town before 10 a.m. on college football gamedays, then Marge certainly wasn't a trailblazer. But, then again, she isn't priming for a game. Unless, that is, the game is life itself.

"Thank you," I responded.

The atmosphere roiled with a depth of dysfunction which I imagined was comparable to an iceberg: perhaps only a small percentage of it was actually showing. There are times as a pastor in which it seems as if I've waded past the breakers into the abyss. This was one of those occasions. I headed for the bedroom.

He was a man of about 80. It was my understanding that he was dying from some type of cancer. This was the first time I had seen him in person. He—along with his wife and his son—allegedly belonged to the congregation to which I was recently called. The social worker had apparently asked Marge if they belonged to a congregation. Marge had forgotten the name, but had given the congregation's cross-streets. The social worker then contacted our congregation's office to indicate that "one of ours" was in dire straits. She indicated that a home visit would be a good idea. We checked our rolls. The family at one time had been "one of ours." They hadn't darkened the church's doorstep in over 30 years. I had my secretary arrange a home visit.

I am reminded of the old-timer at my first call. As was custom, a ministry team from our congregation gathered on a Monday evening to make house calls to those who were unable to frequent worship. He was dying from a host of issues—what they used to call *old age*. He was whittled-down to his last few weeks of life. He was what we affectionately called in those parts "a stubborn old German." He was one of those old barrel-chested farmers whose palms were like baseball gloves. His thick, weathered fingers appeared as a couple handfuls of Cuban cigars. Religion during his life revolved more around the weather, its predictability, than anything else.

After a good half hour of pleasantries, I indicated to him that we had to "move on to our next visit." I then asked him if we could have a short prayer together. His response?

"Sure as hell wouldn't hurt anything." It still hits my funny bone.

But observation and experience has also led me to consider that such words are, for many, the true expression of the church's role in American society: "sure as hell wouldn't hurt anything." It's not exactly an institution freighted with life-determining meaning for many of its members. It often appears to function more in the vein of a congressional chaplain on Capitol Hill: "Thanks for the nice prayer, let's now get back to business." It is not uncommon for pastors to become disheartened by the discrepancy between their passion and idealism and the reality of the church's often subsidiary role in the communities to which they are called.

"Sure as hell wouldn't hurt anything." Those were the words which popped into my mind as I made my way from the kitchen to the bedroom. I sensed—factoring in their relationship to the congregation, along with her words—that such was the significance of my visit on this day. At least from her perspective.

Having entered the bedroom, the first thing I noticed was a newly acquired hospice bed. It was one of those beds that can be adjusted for upper and lower body elevation. The problem was this: whoever delivered the bed didn't bring the guardrails with it. Which created another problem the family haphazardly remedied. Namely, to secure his body from falling out of the bed due to his uncontrollable thrashing, somebody had tied his left hand to the headboard with a small piece of rope. Due to his thrashing and mattress migration, his left arm was perpetually positioned over his head. It was as if gravity was pulling him horizontally from the direction of the footboard. And there were no sheets or blankets on his bed. He was lying on a mattress with a small pillow without its pillow case. The pillow was wedged between the wall the bed. He was in nothing but an adult diaper that had yet to be changed. The fecal smell was suffocating. The scene provoked simultaneously both visceral revulsion and visceral compassion.

Earl was writhing, thrashing in his hospital bed. His words were incoherent. He also communicated a mixture of groans and soft howls. I simply observed him for a solid couple of minutes. Then I spoke his name. I introduced myself. His agony created something of an isolating shell with regard to communication. Nonetheless, I continued to address him. This may have been the first time I have ever given thanks for cigarette smoke. It veiled the fecal smell. I peered back into the kitchen.

"Marge, is anyone coming to install guardrails on Earl's bed?" She indicated that the social worker was coming later that morning to address the issue. She also indicated that the home healthcare nurse was on his way over. Meanwhile the sight was pathetic. It quickly became apparent that my visit, in addition to those of the nurse and the social worker, may have been the only form of dignity he received all day. Perhaps all week

"Marge," I spoke up again, "when was the last time Earl's diaper was changed?"

"Sum-b*^%# was all cleaned up late last night," she responded. "Jackass soil his self again? Sum-b*^%# stinking again? He's comin' soon."

I stepped back over to the bedside. I continued talking to Earl. I caressed his right arm as I spoke to him. Again, I reminded him who I was, where I was from. I referenced the weather. I brought up what little I knew about his background. Anything to connect, for him to hear a friendly voice.

I pulled out my Bible. I read a few passages.

Then I got on my knees, figuring I'd finish this visit with a robust prayer. I grabbed Earl's free hand, his right hand, with my left. Right then his son walked through the door from the kitchen, his dark brown, over-Brylcreemed, thinning hair pulled back, culminating in a small ponytail his hair wasn't thick enough to wear. He was wearing dark blue jeans and a faded black Mötley Crüe t-shirt. A scattered attempt at a mustache donned his upper lip.

"Oh, Father, gawd it's great you're here. Was hopin' to be here when you came. Just got home. Want to join you in prayer."

Certainly, he had to have known that I wasn't a Roman Catholic priest. My clerical collar must have thrown him for a loop. I deduced from his brief, graphic exchange with his mother that he had just arrived home from some type of overnight hook up. His answer to his mother's question as to his nocturnal whereabouts was framed as a graphic description of a sexual encounter with "some gal he had met at the bar."

It wasn't his answer to his mother's question as to his whereabouts that caused my eyebrow to raise. It was her response: "Just be safe." I'm still not sure what a *safe* version of the encounter he described looks like.

He wreaked of booze. His breath smelled like the cleaning supply room at the local public school. Regardless: "Please," I responded.

On my knees and holding his father's right hand in my left, Billy—having descended to his knees, now facing me—placed his left hand in my right. I neglected to tell Billy *how* I would pray. At the same time, there has never been a need for me to inform folks as to how I was going to pray. Or maybe, in retrospect, what was about to unfold was prayer in its most authentic form.

I began to pray. I addressed this concern and that on Earl's behalf. His discomfort made him oblivious to my words. He was thrashing, restive. My prayer turned in the direction of gratitude, gratitude for all the blessings of this life—no matter how well concealed. And it was here that Billy's quiet amens during the first part of the prayer acquiesced into something more colorful, more raw, more memorable.

Facing me, he began addressing petitions to me. His petitions, addressed to me as *Father*, went like this:

"Goddammit, Father, I want your forgiveness. I love that stuff. Unnerstannin' me? what I'm sayin'? Can't get enough. Oh, Father, I can't stop lovin' that stuff. I've had so many I don't remember their names. I'm addicted to that stuff."[1]

I tried to maintain focus. I had never stopped a prayer to correct behavior. I wasn't going to start now. I was somewhere at the intersection of prayerful conviction, embarrassment, and a river of prurient images coursing through my mind. Part of me wanted to stop, ask: are you confessing or bragging? Was this welling up from the depth of sincerity? Memories of my football days were involuntarily conjured. The voice of an old football teammate from college—a Lutheran church college!—came to mind. His broadcast to the underclassmen in the pre-practice locker room regarding his sexual prowess echoed between my ears.

I had moved in the prayer from gratitude to addressing various physical and relational needs. But the prurient part of me couldn't quell the images flooding my mind. This was the first time the Good Shepherd and oral sex have been juxtaposed in my mind. It was, strangely, not as discombobulating as I may have anticipated such a situation to be. I've learned to be merciful with my mind's own libidinous intrusions. I powered forward with the petitions of my prayer. And so did Billy power forward with his petitions.

"I've enjoyed all types. I've enjoyed girlfriends and total strangers. I've done it for beer money. I've had older women. I've had young women. Hell, Father, it's so hard to stop."

And, suddenly, Marge's voice chimed in from the kitchen. And, no, it was not to scold her adult child for indecency. She joined the two petition prayers already in progress with her own petition prayer. And so it became a threesome petition prayer in a smoky, fecal-smelling single-wide.

---

1. I have profoundly toned down his language.

"I pray that sum-b*^%$ get what he deservin'. Dear God, that adulteratin' sum-b*^%$ is reapin' what he's sowed. Sum-b*^%$. He doesn't deserve grace. No grace, pastor." Marge was clearly animated with a deep resentment, a profound pain, that I would not be able to touch.

Meanwhile Billy's petitions continued, now complemented by his mom's newly-commenced petitions. My own petitions garnished this threesome with strands of well-known Bible passages and such words as *grace* and *love* and *healing*. It was a colorful prayer in this raw realm of God's creation.

"Been wondrin' if I have a problem, Father. Gawd I love that stuff, Father."

By no means was Marge's arsenal of petitions depleted. She continued, "Lord knows what an adulteratin', drunkin' sum-b*^%$ Earl is. Doesn't deserve no mercy. Please, no mercy. Bastard."

And again, Billy: "I know I should stop. But I can't get enough of the stuff. Father, it's a gift I have." (I'll return to the concept of *gift*, in a bit.)

Marge chimed in again with another "sum-b*^$#, a$$h*&^"-laced petition . . .

. . . and finally, my voice broke through again: "Surely goodness and mercy will pursue you all the days of your life, and you will dwell in the house of the Lord forever. Amen." And so my prayer was finished. Taking the *amen* as their cue, Billy's and Marge's petitions dwindled to a stop. Obviously, there was religious impulse in this peculiar house of the Lord. *Amen* is universal. In this case it was translated as *prayer is over*.

My first threesome was now finished. As raw, as X-rated as it was, I felt neither unclean nor offended. Just alive. And a bit frazzled. I got off my knees. I made the sign of the cross on Earl's forehead. I turned to shake Billy's hand. "Billy, my door is always open for a conversation, for counsel and prayer."

"Yer a good man, Father."

I remember thinking that if the wife permitted me to return—which she did not—I would be wearing flannel shirt. A *Father* wouldn't wear a flannel shirt for visitation rounds. I departed the bedroom and headed through the kitchen to the exit.

"Thank you, Marge, for permitting me time with Earl. Whatever you need, let me know." I gave her my card to give to the social worker. Taking a gulp of beer from her coffee cup, followed by a long drag from her cigarette, she simply responded, "That sum-b*^%$ hasn't much time. Good Lord knows, ya reap what ya sow." Earl died a couple of weeks later.

I opened the door to the outside. Stepping onto the patio, I looked at my watch. It was 10:15 a.m. The first thing that crossed my mind seemed rather counterintuitive, namely, an ice-cold beer sure sounded good right about then. As well, it occurred to me that all those raw, spirited *petitions* created a strange awareness of how intimacy is expressed in my own marriage.

Certainly, Earl's condition was top of mind. But my thinking revolved around the gifts, the blessings—both the talent and the zeal for that talent—with which Billy had claimed to be gifted. These, too, belong on the divine continuum of blessing. It's only too bad his blessings weren't shared with—in this case—one woman in a committed, intimate relationship of self-giving love.

The continuum of God's gifts, God's blessings, is infinite, one that includes—yes, even—*Billy's gifts*. What separates blessing from curse is not the thing, but its use. It has always been my sense that the "iniquity of the fathers" which is manifested to the "third and fourth generations" (Ex 34:7) has more to with the role-modeling of the usage of God's gifts than the mere handing-down of the gifts themselves.

That home was, in retrospect, among other things certainly, the outcome of a long process of intimacy's exsanguination between husband and wife. And it was the expression of a son who sought the gift of intimacy—perhaps as it had been habitually modeled—among strangers. The gift of intimacy was now boiled-down to an obsessive, objectified, mechanical expression.

But ultimately, as I headed for my car to continue my visitation schedule, another thought came to mind. Namely, no matter how much I needed to process for myself what I had just encountered, the house from which I was leaving was no less capable of the holy, of being holy, than the house in which I officiate Sunday worship. Its crap, quite literally, was simply more out in the open.

I'm not sure what is worse: the holiness we think we've earned or the holiness we're convinced we're not worthy of; the holiness we've identified with virtue or the holiness which we have been convinced tabernacles in a heaven removed from creation. The former cases poison congregations. The latter ones destroy souls.

I've always wondered whether this family, the family I encountered during the visit I just narrated, was trapped in some form of a snowballing bondage to the latter form of logic. It is a feedback loop which reinforces itself, intensifying our imprisonment to our vices, our distorted uses of God's gifts. Amid such captivity we convince ourselves that God's grace—which would humanize us, humanize us to each other—is nothing more than a prison guard of a higher order.

Nonetheless, this visit has served as a reminder that it is the Word of God alone who sanctifies a place, a people, their gifts. Those gifts will either reflect the God who mediates life through them, or become false gods which convince us that they are the goal of life. Ripped from the Grace who gives them freely, who is revealed in and through them, the gifts become our taskmaster. Concretely, the gift of intimacy—its desire—for which God has created us always stirs within. Such a desire can either humanize us and those around us. Or dehumanize us and those around us. If there is one thing our idols convince us to do well . . . it is the latter.

Yet the gifts of the living God, the gifts by which the living God sustains us, though distorted, are not withdrawn.

(3)

Ministering to Dying and Death

The Word is Enough

I was serving as a vicar in their congregation. I was learning the trade, so-to-speak, under my supervising pastor. Due to my skill set my supervisor entrusted me with the lion's share of the congregation's visitation duties that year. It was during that year that I got to know the couple, their kids.

They were both in their mid-30s. They were the parents of three kids—two girls, and boy—ages thirteen, eleven, and seven. The boy was the youngest. I'll call her—the wife—Joanie. I'll call him Derald. If my memory serves me correctly, the couple was from the Midwest. They had moved west and started a family.

I knew family from worship during the year. But it wasn't until a Tuesday afternoon in early March that I got to know them better. Earlier that day our church secretary received a phone call. The family requested for me to come over that afternoon.

Greeted by Derald at the door, he escorted me inside their ranch-style home. Their kids were still at school. Seated in the corner of the room, by the fireplace, was Joanie. I don't remember what she wore. But I can conjure a knitted shawl—blue and white striped—covering her legs. Her right hand, in her lap, was cusping a Kleenex. In her left hand were hospice pamphlets. She had been weeping.

The long and the short of the meeting: Joanie had been diagnosed with stage-4 cancer that had originated somewhere—I forget precisely—in her reproductive organs. The metastases were extensive. The prognosis was one to four months. Near the end of our time together, I scheduled a home communion visit for the following Tuesday. I finished with prayer. Derald walked me out to my car. I reassured him that I would walk with them through the dying process. As we traversed the front walk, Derald wondered out loud about "how much more time she had."

Then Friday evening arrived.

Only a few days had elapsed since I had departed their home. My wife and I were watching a movie, having just arrived home from a dinner out. It had been a long week. It was about 9:30 p.m. The phone rang. Obviously, I thought, this must be family from back home, or a friend who lived down the road. Who else calls a vicar at 9:30 p.m. on a Friday night?

I walked to the kitchen and picked up the phone.

"Hello?"

"Vicar, this is Derald," he paused, his voice was quiet. His words seemed like they were emanating from a thousand miles away. He added, "Joanie took a turn this afternoon. She's gone."

"O God, Derald, I'm so sorry." I continued, "Where are you?"

"We're at home." He paused, "She's still here. Would you be able to come out here for a prayer?"

"Absolutely, Derald. Give me twenty minutes."

They lived in another town a handful of miles away. It was one of those rare occasions in which I didn't need either a jolt of coffee or a few minutes to arrange an emotional segue. The car ride over to the house would be my jolt and my segue.

"Give me a couple of hours," I told my wife, "Joanie died." My wife was understanding. I warned her the previous Tuesday evening this may happen. But certainly—I had thought—not in a few days.

It took a handful of minutes to get past the city limits, out into the open desert between the two communities. It was night and the light of desert moon had caused the contours of the desert mountains to come into sharper relief. The desert has always seemed magically alive at night. I was on my way to minister in an atmosphere of death. I remember wondering what she would look like. It had only been three days since I had last seen her.

"That's not her," declared an aunt. "That doesn't look like Mom at all."

The whole family—my parents, aunts and uncles, cousins—was in the viewing room at the mortuary getting its first opportunity to view my grandmother. She died from non-Hodgkin's lymphoma after five years of carpet-bombing, er, chemotherapy. I was sixteen.

It was as if we were standing around a new model of automobile which we were eagerly awaiting to be unveiled. The family stood in a semi-circle before the casket when the funeral director lifted the casket's lid.

As soon as the lid was raised, like the shock wave of a bomb blast moving across the landscape, a renewed round of palpable grief flooded over the family. It was as if Grandma had died all over again.

There she lay, a tallish-lady of mostly *Slesviger* stock (as we have come to learn), silverish-blonde hair nicely done, mouth unnaturally closed, hands clasped at her waist. She was clothed in a metallic blue dress with a thin, dark blue belt.

This was not the Grandma I last saw, cancer consuming her body, pain personified and peering from her eyes. Embalmed bodies remind me of a kitchen table still-life, one of those starving artist depictions of fruit—oranges, apples, and the like. Both are artist's depictions equally incapable of animation.

A parishioner in his early nineties declared that, over the age of seventy-five, all embalmed bodies look the same. That thought detains me more than it probably should. Perhaps it's a reminder that death obliterates identity. So, your grandma died in her mid-80s with little collagen, thin hair, and no eye brows? Produce a picture for the funeral home of Grandma in her late sixties and let the artist get to work. The bones are the scaffold. The paper-thin skin is canvas. Now ask the artist to produce a piece of work that won't emblazon on our memory the wages of aging, disease, and death.

Having stared as a family for several minutes at Grandma, an aunt then stepped forward to impugn the embalmer's work. She was incensed. It became infectious.

"That's not Mom!" she declared. "Goddammit, that's not Mom! They made a mistake!" Several times she repeated her discovery.

And then, one by one, the rest of the family like dominoes—fused by emotion—validated her claim. First, my cousin. Then, my great uncle. After that, another cousin. Mutiny in the viewing room!

And then my mom—God bless her, she was brilliant that way—spoke up, her voice cutting the through the cacophony of family hysteria.

She simply asked a question: "Guys, when in the hell did you ever see Mom with her mouth closed?!"

"Huh?" seemed to be the collective reaction, as if on cue.

"When in the hell did Mom ever have her mouth closed? She was always talking!"

No better tool than humor to break the news that embalmers don't inject animation. They only prepare a body to be a parable of the living one. Animation is sacred. Without the breath of God you have stone, mannequins. You have still life portraits of fruit.

Laughter broke out. Indignation acquiesced into a collective ownership of grief which morphed into an atmosphere of stories, laughter, gratitude. The stage was set for a night of fellowship and the sharing of family stories.

I made the turn into their neighborhood. A right, then a quick left. Derald and Joanie's (or just Derald's now?) house was the second house on the right. The driveway seemed to be approaching me, not I it.

What would I see? How would the home be arranged? Who would be there? Would the kids be there? What would Joanie look like? The questions of a young vicar.

I served as a chaplain at a large trauma hospital in Southern California. It was during the summer prior to my internship. I served during the afternoons on both the late-stage oncology and the pediatric intensive care units. Death was omnipresent that summer. Those who died that summer were either over the age of sixty or under the age of fifteen. You never knew, when paged to a room, what to expect, what you would see.

On the pediatric intensive care unit, many of the rooms were filled with young patients whose trauma wounds were profound, often irreversible. Patients were often sedated. Which meant: through daily rounds you got to know the families, but not the patients. Families were often in limbo about when to pull life support. Or which organs they would permit to be harvested.

Emblazoned in my mind's eye—as if it were yesterday—is the twelve-year-old girl who had been hit by a delivery truck while she was skateboarding. She was a beautiful girl with light skin and freckles and brown curls covering her temples and forehead. And she was braindead. The lead chaplain invited me to sit in with both him and the organ harvester as they broached the idea of permitting Nicole's organs to give life beyond her own.

I'll never forget her dad's response: "You can take anything you want. Below the eyes."

I can't put his logic into precise words. Perhaps because such words come from a place deeper than logic. But I get it.

She would be in her late-30s now. The world is flooded with absence.

And every now and again, I was able to develop a relationship with a young person over the course of days and weeks.

I was able to develop a relationship with Shelley, a thirteen-year-old leukemia patient who was in and out of the unit during my first month of my chaplaincy. She was a beautiful, vibrant, young Hispanic woman. She possessed a radiant, infectious smile. Her gorgeous, thick, coal-black, shoulder-length hair was gone, leaving her head bald with small patches of black down. Her face was swollen, perhaps from some type of steroid. She was dying. No denying it. She knew it.

I came to learn that she lived in the community in which I would be working as a vicar. I came to learn that her grandmother was raising her. She had little in the way of family. I never saw them on the unit. We would chat about being a teenager, about life in that "in between world" between childhood and adulthood. We would chat about school, what she liked to study, what kind of career she wanted. She told me about how she wanted to impact the world. It was going to be through medicine that she would change the world.

It was a white-washed Tuesday afternoon. I had just stepped inside her hospitable room. A technician was standing to the right of her bed disentangling cords and moving monitors, his back to me. His presence was so mundane, so matter of fact, that it seemed as if nothing out of the ordinary had just occurred in the room.

Without fanfare, without family, earlier that hour, she died. Alone. The room left no traces of her hopes and dreams; of the beautiful, burning core of her personality. Her corpse gave no trace of the personality which had illuminated it. Her head was tilted to her right, her mouth slightly ajar, just enough to see her teeth. A tube—this last piece of the hospital—was still in her nose, secured by tape. Her eyes were opened a sliver, enough to create a look of perpetual sleepiness. Her powder blue hospital pajamas were covered with a robe of darker blue. What makes death so disturbing at times is that it doesn't seem out of the ordinary. It can seem very ordinary. Routinely ordinary. So ordinary it's jarring.

Not noticing me, the technician tossed some cords he had bundled. He had aimed for the pile of cords already on the chair on the other side of the bed. He missed. They landed on Shelley.

It wasn't until the cords landed short of their mark—dropping into her lap, an event that seemed to magnify the deadness of the deceased—that the technician noticed me. Ironically, recognizing the insensitivity at what had just occurred, he apologized to *me*. I acted like I had not registered what had happened.

A feeling of resentment immediately coursed through my body. The thought gripped me: "Dammit, this is a human being, she is sacred. Watch what you're doing. Don't you have any respect?" But it also occurred to me: "He was indifferent. That's all it was, nothing more. It was an indifference caused by his removal of countless cords and gadgets from many rooms of dead patients throughout his days of work. Regardless, such indifference cannot subtract significance and sacredness from this young lady's life. And neither would his extra care somehow sanctify this young lady's life." This room was the sacred space of solidarity with the crucified Christ. It shimmered with the silence of such solidarity.

I pulled into the driveway. I quickly prayed. I then got out of the car and headed for the front door. Arriving at the front door, I gently rapped on it a couple of times. Derald answered within moments. He greeted me with an embrace. No words were exchanged as he quietly led me into the front room. A hospital bed had been placed in the middle of the front room at some point after my first visit. Joanie, covered in a thin white sheet up to her shoulders, was its occupant.

Her short, sandy-brown hair had been combed. Her eyes had been closed. Her arms had been placed at her side outside the white sheet. But they had been unable to close her mouth. Her tongue appeared desiccated and shriveled. She looked like a dehydrated, smaller version of the Joanie I had just visited on Tuesday afternoon.

Her parents, in their late fifties, were seated together on a love seat to the left of Joanie. Her father's white, wavy hair and beard, his blue flannel shirt, corresponding red suspenders, and blue jeans reminded me of so many men I'd grown up around in the Midwest. He was in the throes of a grief whose presentation he was attempting to manage. Her mother looked like an older version of her daughter. Sitting on her husband's right, she clung to him with her left arm, as if a hurricane was preparing to blow through the house.

I made my way around the foot of the bed to greet her parents. They had just arrived from the Midwest. We hugged. And, working my way farther around her bed—counter-clockwise—were her two girls. I hugged both. I spoke no words. As a grown man—at least at that point—I still had both of my parents. I couldn't pretend to fathom the nature of their loss. It was the loss of a mother yes, but a mother who would not steer them through adolescence, their first dates, their high school experiences, their possible engagements, and wedding days.

Coming around to Joanie's right side, next to Derald, I was offered a metal folding chair. I placed it next to her bed, down by her hips. But I remained standing—near her shoulders—so that I could hold Joanie's hands within mine, caress her arms and her shoulders. My intent was, as it remains now as an older pastor, to remind the family that even in death the deceased is one of us. Even in death she remained within our communion. Even in death she could be loved, caressed, and served. The ministry of Jesus Christ is the revelation of a God who not only transgresses the boundary between divine and human, but has transgressed the boundary between death and life to include us in God's abundant life. Such a ministry calls us to demonstrate such transgressions.

I gently caressed Joanie's shoulders and arms for several minutes. In a silent room it seemed much longer. Then I sat down in the folding chair. It was then that I noticed that their youngest, their little boy, was absent.

"Where is your boy?" I softly asked Derald.

"He's in his room.," Derald replied. "He won't come out. We've tried a couple of times to get him out here to say goodbye to his mom. I can try again," he added.

"No," I softly insisted. "Let's not do that. We don't want to compound his trauma. He'll have time between now and the funeral to see his mother, to talk to her, to say goodbye." "But," I continued, "for the time being, tonight, right now, it'd be good to check on him every handful of minutes or so. That's a good way to keep him connected to the family while letting the grief wash over him."

We sat in a circle around Joanie for some minutes. At first in silence. Then her mother—with a comment—signaled it was ok to converse. "Her face looks peaceful." Her mother's words were the green light for conversation. A few stories about her childhood were told. Then ones about their marriage. And ones about what she was like as a mother. Soon there was a bit a laughter.

And then more silence.

That silence was my cue: I asked for the family to stand around her bed. I requested that each member of the family, according to their level of comfortability, lay a hand on Joanie. Then I prayed a prayer of commendation. We concluded with the Lord's Prayer. When people ask me why I have large sections of the Bible committed to memory I tell them that it is for occasions like this.

With another round of embraces conducted, Derald escorted me out. We briefly spoke about funeral details, about communicating with one another in the days ahead. But Derald didn't simply accompany me to the door. He escorted me down his front walk. Ultimately, he accompanied me to my car.

"Something's on your mind, Derald. What is it?" I asked.

"Pastor, I need to share this with you. It's got me and the family freaked out, kinda scared, to be honest."

"What is it?"

"Do you have a few minutes?"

"I have all the time we need."

"Ok, well, you know pastor, as she was getting closer, she was movin' around more and more, like she couldn't find a comfortable position. And then she said she had pain first in one part of her body, then another, as if it was movin' around in her body, kinda like a 'whack-a-mole.' As instructed by the hospice nurse earlier, we gave her the prescribed morphine." Derald paused, then continued, "But then her breaths got shorter and shorter. And she yelled several times that she couldn't breathe . . . 'please help me, somebody help me, I can't breathe.'"

It seemed like Derald and I were the only two people in the universe.

"Pastor, I can't get those words, that voice, that plea, out of my head . . . 'please help, somebody help me, I can't breathe.' I have never felt as helpless. But that wasn't it . . ."

Derald continued, "Just a few moments before she passed, her eyes got big, and then they were fixed to the end of her bed, as if there was something standing at the foot of her bed, and then she yelled 'Get them out of here, get them away from me, they're ugly. They're scaring me, get them away from me they're ugly.' Then she gasped for breath a few times. Then there was silence. She was gone."

Derald looked up at me and asked, "Pastor, what was it? What was going on? What was she seein'? Should I be worried?"

Such a question provokes a temptation, namely, to be more than a pastoral care giver; to not "stay in my lane" of vocation. That is, I could have said "Well, Derald, it was just the medication playing tricks on Joanie." (Does this then mean it is his fault for administering too much palliative medicine?) Or I could have said, "Derald, it was just due to a decreasing amount of oxygen in her brain." (Does this mean that everything can be reduced to material cause?) Or I could have said, "Yes, Derald, those were demons at the foot of the bed. I hope it all turned it out well for Joanie, that her faith was strong." (As bat-s*^# crazy as it sounds, no doubt some alleged clergyperson has expressed such a logic.)

I'm reminded of a local youth minister. He served at a local community church near my home. He conducted a funeral for my daughter's classmate. Her classmate was profoundly physically challenged. The little lad was bound to a wheel chair, unable to speak, unable to feed himself. At the time of his death, he was eight-years-old. During the sermon the youth minister declared to those in attendance—parents and family, classmates, parents of classmates, teachers—that the little guy's "developmental deformities were caused by the sins of the parents." My eight-year-old daughter—who made sure to eat lunch with this classmate each day, to assist him in eating—turned to my wife and simply said, "Mom, I'm glad Dad preaches the Love of God."

At times I hope that God metes out to that youth minister the "sins of the parents." He'll be surprised at the invoice. Then I remind myself: we both bear, are created in, the image of Christ. God justifies the ungodly. The fundamentalist ungodly. And the mainline ungodly.

I paused, and looked Derald squarely in the eyes. "Derald," I replied, "I don't know what she was seeing. Were they demons? We'll never know. But all I can tell you is this: Nothing will separate Joanie from the presence and love of Jesus Christ our Lord. Nothing."

The words seemed so small. So rote and rehearsed. So simple. But they were enough.

A look of relief migrated across his face. His eyebrows lifted. "Thank you," he responded. We embraced a final time that night.

At the core of my vocation is the promise that the Word is enough.

To want to say more, to think one must say more to speak with authority, may well mean that the God revealed in Jesus Christ is not the personality underwriting one's ministry. But the question has never gone away: were the demons the real? Or something of physiological attribution? The Word of God is enough on either count.

(4)

Funeral Visitation

A Casket Crawler

In the funeral business they are called "casket crawlers." Another term I've heard is "coffin climbers." I had heard rumors of them from funeral directors, usually over coffee during that interval between funeral set-up and the arrival of family. "Too strange to be true," I always thought to myself. Until the day of Fred's funeral. It was during the viewing prior to his funeral, to be precise, that I had an encounter with one.

The widow had requested a one-hour window for open casket visitation before the funeral. The deceased was a man who had died suddenly from a misadventure in his early forties. He was a rugged individualist, a short, wiry man with jet-black hair.

Having grown up in the community in which I was serving, and having fled from it after he had graduated high school, he returned in his 30s to settle down. He married a local gal in his late-thirties. The years between his departure from the community and his return was an interval to which the community had no access. Such an opacity of biographical narrative did not sit well for people who want to *know*.

Subsequently, a politely-vicious atmosphere of gossip had commenced upon word of his sudden death. It revolved around the dark interval between his departure and return to the community, those mysterious, twenty-something years in which identities are forged. Having

FUNERAL VISITATION

gone over the community's horizon during this time, certainly—it had to be the case, according to many—he had succumbed to the spell of darkness. Besides, how else could he have amassed such wealth? And, it was implied, such wandering had a direct relation to his demise. Why else would someone die like *that*? Such a community does not need a story to be true to be told. It is often the case in a community like this that a story's purpose is not the conveyance of truth.

The speculation regarding this period of his life, certainly reinforced by his aloofness, was extravagant to say the least: "He was a bookie," or "He was a drug runner," or—perhaps the funniest one—"He did some work in the adult film industry." Simple psychology, I know, but I suspect that last speculation was projected prurience.

My sense was that he was just a man who, during this interval of time, was trying to figure life out. Should not all of us have a period of our lives to which to no one else has access? But our lives are not Facebook pages. That is, there is no *private* setting when it comes to who can view our lives. Or who can *comment* on them.

We often learn to bury that interval in which we transformed our demons into life-serving angels. But here is the problem: it is not who we become that most intrigues people, but the adversities through which we have struggled. To see who we've become requires people to *see* us without framing us by our past. Framed, identified, by those around us for past decisions and actions, it easy to become a self-reenforcing temple of shame. It is the struggles of life which have most shaped us, gifted us wisdom, which have forged meaning and purpose. Yet we are somehow convinced that shame should overshadow the growth we have gleaned from them. Did Fred want this interval hidden? Was it a dark interval? Better, did he have any control over the matter?

At the time of his death, he had only been married a small handful of years. His wife worked in an office in a larger town up the highway. His sudden, unexpected death ended a marriage which had essentially just begun.

The funeral service was expected to be a big one. Factoring the man's age and the wife's connections, this was no doubt going to be a funeral that utilized every inch of our worship and worship overflow space.

Though there would be a viewing the night before, the widow requested that there also be an open-casket visitation one hour prior to service time. The widow—along with her parents and siblings—would form a greeting line near the casket. Such was the plan for the day of the funeral.

My secretary had just hung up the phone, flustered, and let out an "oh hell" to the count of a whole note. "What's up?" I asked. The secretary was in the office across the hallway.

"Pastor, Sharon just called. She drove by the church today, to make sure the lawn had been mowed by the property committee, and now her underwear is in a bunch. You know what the problem now is, Pastor? It's the goddamned dandelions."

She continued, "I swear to God, if it's not one thing, it's another. She's the kind of person who'd b*^%# and moan were she to be hanged with a new rope. People like that live to be one hundred years old."

I responded, "What do you mean by 'the goddamned dandelions'? What is she referring to?"

My secretary shot back, "Three of 'em. In the church yard. Behind the electronic church sign. Three goddamned dandelions. Apparently, her husband's funeral will be shot all to hell if those dandelions are still there by the beginning of the service tomorrow afternoon."

Sharon was the gal who, when I posted my office hours, made sure to check that they were precisely kept. Sharon was the gal who, having circled the typos in the Sunday announcements and worship order, left them—no name attached, of course—in the secretary's church mail box. Sharon was the gal who comprised our church's one person altar guild. Sharon was the gal who, when funeral luncheons were conducted, took over the church kitchen. She took it upon herself to tell the other women whether their desserts were *acceptable* or not.

"How in the hell," I thought to myself, "with all the traffic going by the building in this city, with all the flowers dotting the church campus's landscape, did she notice *that*?"

"What should we do, Pastor?" asked my secretary. She quickly quipped, "Should we leave 'em just to spite? Perhaps we could pick 'em and bundle 'em with some Baby's Breath and make a funeral arrangement out of 'em." We laughed. Such ideas were funny to consider. They diffused frustration.

Ultimately, those dandelions had to be picked. At the same time, no number of picked dandelions was going to bring order to the chronic chaos of her life. The next day we would be burying her husband, a man whose alcoholism had come to full bloom, flowering deep into his body and his family. Those goddamned dandelions had deep roots.

FUNERAL VISITATION

The day of Fred's funeral arrived. It was a beautiful spring day, no clouds in sight. A light shower had come through during the night. The funeral was scheduled to begin at 1 p.m., as was customary in this congregation.

The family arrived fifteen minutes before noon to have some time alone in the sanctuary before the open casket. Upon arrival they slowly filed up to the casket which the funeral director had just opened. The casket was situated at the front of the sanctuary, just in front of the steps to the chancel. It sat between the chancel and the first row of pews which were separated by a center aisle. The grief was just as intense, but less audible than the previous evening when the family viewed Fred for the first time.

The funeral service for her husband was just about to begin. The funeral director had indicated to Loretta, a woman in her early-60s, that she had a final opportunity to view her husband—a man who had died suddenly of a heart attack—before the casket was closed for good.

Sobbing, she stood over his body. She caressed his hands. As she loosened his tie a bit, she said, "You can't be comfortable with it being so tight." She gently massaged his forehead. "You'll be ok," she said, "We'll get through this."

She then turned, reached into her purse, and pulled out a comb. She placed it in her husband's shirt pocket.

And then she pulled out a devotional prayer booklet and placed it in his hands.

She then, having excused herself briefly, went to her car and quickly returned with a quilt which she placed in his casket, covering his abdomen. "I don't want him to get cold," she stated.

Then, having gone into the back of the sanctuary, returned, and placed both a hymnal and pew Bible in his casket.

A squall-line of panic began to creep across the funeral director's face. I stepped forward and gently reminded her that we would need to be able to close the casket. I also reminded her that the service was to begin in a handful of minutes. She stopped her casket packing.

But not before talking her great grandson—perhaps three or four at the time—out of his teddy bear, which, she convinced him, "would be of great comfort to papa." Into the casket it went. I have always wondered whether that youngster had to be dragged to funerals after that. Perhaps the only thing more traumatic than death is adults in the agony of its denial.

The time had arrived for the general visitation to occur. The family had formed a greeting line near the casket. Members of the community began filing in. The sanctuary started to fill up. I was standing by the entrance to the sanctuary, my back to the family. I was chatting with the funeral director. Such conversations—at this point in time, just before the funeral—often revolve around service details and logistics.

About fifteen minutes into the visitation, interrupting our conversation, the funeral director, pointing to the casket, simply said, "I think you have some business to attend to." I turned. "What the hell" were the only words that went through my mind. What filled my gaze was surreal.

On the matter of surreal memories . . . I am reminded of the time, after taking a long, reflective walk on a beautiful Southern California beach with my internship supervisor—we were given a dinner break during a retreat for interns and their supervisors—when we stumbled upon an adult film set in the middle of shooting a scene. We couldn't not go by it within feet. To get back to the car we had to walk between a small cliff to our left and the ocean to our right. The film set was on our right, between us and the ocean. At first, I didn't comprehend what I was looking at. And then, by the time we reached the car, I did. But who is shameless enough to take a second pass for confirmation?

I'll never forget the question the retreat leader asked our group when we returned from our dinner break: "Did you do or see anything interesting?"

The scene was jarring. What filled my gaze was this: a middle-aged woman, perhaps in her late 40s, with long, carrot-red hair. She wore a long, tan, cotton wrap-around skirt with knee-high boots, and a black blouse with long sleeves. She had managed to damn-near climb into Fred's casket. One foot—her right—was off the ground. The casket stand was essentially supporting both Fred and her.

Her chest was pressed against his. Her hands had enveloped his face. Her lips, as evidenced by the lipstick trail, had been all over his face. They resembled bunny tracks.

"Oh no," I thought to myself, "how long has this been going on?" I quickly made my way down the center aisle to address the issue. Fred's widow and her family were just feet away from the spectacle.

As I approached it was clear that I was intruding on an unrequited declaration of love: "My sweet prince, gawd you were the best . . . your body, your lips, your laugh . . . Remember the times we made love until the sunrise? Remember all the things we . . ."

"You're done," I said, having arrived at the casket. Simultaneously, I had placed my hands on her shoulders to begin the process of pulling her out of the casket.

Her feet back on the ground, she quickly turned around, looked me squarely in the eye with a scowl on her face, and said, "Who the f&*$ are you?!" I was wearing a black suit with my black clerical shirt. Apparently, she needed more clues as to my identity.

"Get your f&*$^*# hands off me!" she added.

"It's time to go, you've forgotten where you're at, you've outstayed your welcome," I asserted in matter-of-fact fashion.

In the manner of a butler directing guests to the smoking room, I gestured with my left arm to the door. She took a deep, passive-aggressive, audible breath and began to walk down the aisle toward the entrance to the sanctuary. But she was not done talking. The sanctuary was filling up and she, not Fred or Fred's widow, had become the central feature.

"You need to know, and I don't care who the f&*$ I'm talking to, that you're the worst priest I've ever known. In fact, you're just a f&*$%*^ a**h^%# . . . won't let a woman grieve . . . interrupt a person in mourning . . . who the f&*$ are you?! F&*$ you."

Escorting her down the center aisle of the sanctuary seemed like eternity in slow motion. "Smile, and just keep walking," I thought to myself. In the process of guiding her out, I managed to communicate a few silent hellos—using my eyebrows and other facial gestures—to newly arrived parishioners and members of the community.

Moving past the sanctuary doors out into the narthex, she added, "You better f&*%$^# believe nobody I know is gonna hear a good word about this hellhole called a church. You just keep serving these hypocrites you son of a b*^$#."

Arriving at the front door, I slipped around her to open the left side of the double door for her. She passed by me into the sunlight and fresh air. Taking about ten steps, she turned and made one final communication, a hand gesture. I interpreted it to mean that I was "#1" in her heart. I'm still working on interpreting hand gestures.

I made my way back into the sanctuary. The funeral director was delicately removing lipstick from Fred's face. He had combed his hair back into place. I made a beeline for the widow. I was now in uncharted waters on the matter of pastoral care. Never had I been given advice about ministering in the aftermath of a "casket crawler."

Later, in the days following the service, I learned that this "casket crawler" was a specter conjured from the world of his twenties, from that interval of life we hope serves to shape us rather than become the shape of us. She was proof that the present is permeable to the past.

Not only was the widow dealing with his sudden death—the *why*—but now she was forced to come to terms with a past which didn't remain irretrievably past. It was as if she was forced to mourn two deaths, one physical/relational in nature, the other of an image. It is an image—acquired through growth—which we pray remains in place long after we have any power to define our life's official narrative. The "casket crawler" was a guarantee that any interpretation of his life would not simply begin with his mid-30s, his marriage, or where the arc of his life was bending. It would include, as well, the project's raw materials.

There was a time when I chuckled at the thought of such things as "casket crawlers." I once consigned them to a category containing such entities as the Loch Ness Monster, Big Foot, and honest politicians: widely discussed but rarely observed. But "casket crawlers" are unquestionably real. When you first lay eyes on one, they can be a bit disorienting. Life entering a casket can have an unnerving effect on the senses. But this "casket crawler" was a potent *aide-mémoire* that in our deaths we don't just lose our lives, we lose control of how those lives are presented and interpreted.

On the matter of our neighbor Martin Luther asserted, "We are to fear and love God, so that we do not tell lies about our neighbors, betray or slander them, or destroy their reputations. Instead, we are to come to their defense, speak well of them, and interpret everything they do in the best possible light."[1] Especially in death. Death does not exempt our neighbors from this expression of love.

Indeed, our words are to reflect the promise that our lives—the lives of those around us—are not to be interpreted through any other lens than the promise of Jesus Christ who fashions us unto new creation. May the story of that promise be the story which suppresses all others, which defines us, when death arrives.

---

1. Luther, "The Small Catechism," 353.

(5)

Preaching

Too much goddamn Grace!

His outburst came midway through the worship service. Specifically, it came near the end of my sermon.

The sermon that day was based on Luke 13:6–9, the "Parable of the Barren Fig Tree." I developed the point that the vineyard owner had a fig tree planted smack dab in the middle of his cash crop of grapes. I developed the point that the fig tree—which had been planted merely for the sake of the vineyard owner's love of figs—was barren of its only reason for existing. I developed the point that this fruitless—for three years!—fig tree was taking up valuable cash crop space. I underscored the point that the vineyard owner wanted it chopped down. Enter the gardener.

"Sir," the gardener responded to the vineyard owner, "let it be" (*aphes*) for one more year, until I dig around it and put manure on it. If it bears fruit next year, well and good; but if not, you can cut it down" (Luke 13:8). Stepping into the breach between the vineyard owner and the fruitless fig tree, the gardener committed himself singlehandedly to the preservation of the fig tree's life. Note: we are never told in this short parable whether the fig tree ultimately bore fruit. Perhaps the withholding of such information intensifies the depth of the gardener's commitment.

By now it may be obvious (or it may not be) that the vineyard owner is God the Father, the gardener is Jesus Christ, and the barren fig tree is humanity. Created on the sixth day to reflect God's image in the temple of creation (Gen 1:26), to bear the "fruits of the Spirit" (see Gal 3:22–23), humanity is found by the vineyard owner to be perennially wanting of its raison d'être. So the gardener stepped between the fig tree and the vineyard owner to declare, "let it alone!" As in: "I am now responsible for the life of this barren fig tree!"

That same gardener, suspended from the cross, declared to his Father—on behalf of those who betrayed, denied, abandoned, fled, chanted for execution, and carried out murder—"Let them be (*aphes*); they do not know what they are doing" (Luke 23:34). "Their lives are now bound up with my mercy." We are provided a future from such inexhaustible mercy.

Just before I reached the end of the sermon, I related Jesus' teaching on forgiveness—"Not seven times, but, I tell you, seventy-times seven" (Matt 18:21).[1]—to the results I had harvested from my development of the "Parable of the Barren Fig Tree." "Our mercy, our forgiveness is inexhaustible" I asserted, "because it is an expression of the God from whom, in whom, we live and have our being."

At this point, sitting about ten rows back near the aisle, on the pulpit side of the sanctuary, he erupted.

I had just conducted a funeral for a man I had never known. The local funeral home had called earlier that week. I was asked if I was available to officiate a funeral for a veteran. "Absolutely," I responded. The funeral home gave me the contact information for the widow so that we could plan the service. It would be conducted at the funeral home. I met with widow, along with one of her daughters, the next day to discuss such matters as music, Bible readings, order of service, and eulogists. Eventually, I covered the service of committal, what to expect as to its content and duration. Since the deceased was a veteran, I detailed the military rite which would be performed. For pastors who are liturgical sticklers, this rite comes before the service of committal.

The day of the funeral came. The service was finished and we had processed out of the funeral home's sanctuary. The casket had been loaded into the hearse for the brief trip across the cemetery grounds for the service of committal. I was waiting for the processional car to arrive under the funeral home's awning. It was there that the other daughter encountered me.

---

1. The number seven is symbolic for completion, perfection, and/or wholeness. The implication: as God's mercy is inexhaustible, so forgiveness is inexhaustible.

"Pastor," she said, extending her hand, "thank you for conducting the service for my father."

"It has been a privilege," I responded.

"But," she added, "I was extremely disappointed that you didn't say more in your talk about the greatness of our country's armed forces."

Now, certainly, you must know, I give thanks for those who have served in the United States Armed Forces. I come from a family of proud military service. My own father was awarded the Bronze Star for actions in South Vietnam. But . . .

Thank God for an internal editor. At the beginning of my ministry I would have expressed defensiveness, perhaps briefly explained the purpose of a Christian funeral service, its funeral sermon. Perhaps I might have indicated to her that my words in the middle of the service weren't simply a *talk*, as if they were merely one person's opinions on religion, but indeed the proclamation of the resurrection promise. I didn't explain that I didn't know her father, or serve in the military, but that neither *deficiency* affected the veracity of the *talk*.

I smiled. And I simply said with an upbeat voice, "That's too bad. But the best is yet to come." She gave me a confused look and walked away.

The resurrection promise is proclaimed where the institutions, its instruments, of crucifixion are celebrated. For many Jesus becomes a nice blessing for such rites.

He was not a member of the congregation I served. He had been coming to worship with his lady friend. She was a member of the congregation. As with all new faces, I made a point of learning his name and background. I made a point of visiting with him during coffee hour following worship.

In one of our earliest conversations—and at the time it struck me as odd—he asked me my opinion of Anselm of Canterbury, the well-known Benedictine theologian of the eleventh/early twelfth centuries. Anselm of Canterbury was known for such matters as his argument for the existence of God and his atonement theory. I don't remember the answer I gave. But it was clearly important—as the tone of his voice made clear—that I be made aware that Anselm of Canterbury was his favorite theologian from church history. Never before or since has Anselm of Canterbury been mentioned during a church fellowship hour. I would soon discover that I had been handed an important insight into his personality. I'll return to Anselm of Canterbury—a simplified sketch of his atonement theory—shortly.

I learned that he was a professional in the health industry. Originally from another state, he had worked in the nearest town for many years. He also had two grown children. His daughter had a family and lived in another state. She was a professional. His praise of her was endless. His son was a different matter entirely. Any questions posed about his son caused his focus to shift to such matters as the nature of grace and the limits of forgiveness.

Eventually, having worshiped with us for a month, he handed me an article during fellowship hour. It was snipped from what appeared to be a smalltown newspaper. It was an advice column authored by some species of minister with "Reverend" before his name. He had circled with red ink the first of the two letter/responses.

A man had written "Reverend" seeking advice on how to deal with his son's predicament. He suffered from an addiction which led him to committing grand larceny to keep it funded. And his arrest led to the police finding drugs in his possession. He had been prosecuted and incarcerated. The father's question for "Reverend" was simply: how do I forgive my son for his addiction, his crimes, his incarceration?

"Reverend's" advice was this: withhold forgiveness and alienate him until he has demonstrated what you (the father, in this case) consider to be proper contrition. Because, "Reverend" added, the son has done more than use drugs, commit crimes, and become incarcerated. He has brought shame on your house and your name. And because of that shame he must feel the full nature of God's discipline.

The issue was not—according to "Reverend"—a young man mired in the vicious web of addiction. The matter was not about a young man alienated from family and community, broken in body and spirit. The focus was not on a young man crying out for healing, grasping in the dark for a wholeness which couldn't be swallowed, smoked, or injected. The issue was simply: the son has brought shame to the family, specifically, to the father. And the father's honor must be restored. Such was the advice of "Reverend."

According to Anselm of Canterbury—obviously a simplistic reading of his atonement theory—the crucifixion of God the Son satisfies the debt created when God's honor was compromised by human sin. In the death of Jesus Christ is the restoration of God's honor, a debt satisfied in humanity's place. Essentially, God demands a pound of flesh for God's honor to be satisfied and God's justice to be restored.

But let us ask: how does worship of a God who demands a pound of flesh to satisfy God's honor and restore justice translate into the lives of Christians? What are the implications when such a divine logic is internalized? I was learning the answer face to face. The father who had given me "Reverend's" advice column was making a point. He was telling me something about his circumstances and his mind.

"If what you want from a sermon is three anecdotes and a pearl of advice for life's problems, I'm not your person." That was my response to the call committee when they asked about my preaching style. Undoubtedly it came off chippy. It wasn't intended as such. But, having been through the call process multiple times, I would rather err on the direct side of the spectrum than take a chance on giving any false impressions about my understanding of the role of a sermon.

Rarely do I give advice from the pulpit. Advice is what I give in counseling. I don't preach bullet point sermons from the pulpit with fill-in-the-blank outlines handed out to the assembly. In my opinion, the Gospel narrative—its employment of irony, the subversive nature of the kingdom's revealing, its implication for each listener—doesn't lend itself well to simple outlines. I don't advocate political positions and platforms from the pulpit, either. No, not because of a desire to "separate church and state." The kingdom of God has profound implications for how we conduct ourselves within the political realm. I don't advocate political positions and platforms because—in the words of one of my old professors—"the crucified One is the outcropping on which all ideologies come to a shipwreck." I am called to confront idolatries, especially ideological ones, not perpetuate them.

I do advocate for justice from the pulpit. If that justice is grounded in the narrative of the crucified and risen Jesus Christ who confronts and embraces his victimizers. I will not baptize justice in the form of retribution.

From the pulpit, navigating biblical text and congregational context, it is my intent to speak the Gospel—in countless ways—that "Now, apart from the law, the justice of God has been revealed" (Rom 3: 21); that now, in the crucified and risen Christ, "the mystery that has been hidden throughout the ages and generations . . . has been revealed to his saints" (Col 1: 26). I stress the word *intent* because, frankly, it—*preaching*—is difficult.

Bursting up from his seat he declared, "Too much goddamn grace!" He then stormed down the aisle, out of the sanctuary, out of the church building. He left his lady friend in the pew. His performance was conducted before 118 Sunday worshipers. Upon his outburst and exit I paused a couple of beats. I waited for a parting remark. Which never came. I then finished the sermon. Other than a few quizzical looks, the service continued as usual.

His lady friend remained in the pew. Her head was turned down. For the remainder of the service she remained in a universe of floor inspection, even when she came to the altar rails to receive Communion. Eventually, when the service was finished, she came through the greeting line.

"Gladys," I said, holding my hand out, "it is so good to see you today. Please give my best to Sam." Her gaze briefly met mine. Then, as if drawn by a magnet, her eyes went back to the floor. I reached out to her several times after that service. No calls were ever returned.

The benediction had been spoken and I had just processed down the aisle. Making it just beyond the doors of the funeral home's chapel, I stopped. A stentorian voice could be heard from the chapel I had just departed. "What's going on?" I thought to myself. "Did I forget something?" I listened intently.

The voice was that of the widower. And I couldn't believe what I was hearing. I looked back into the chapel. He was standing in front of his wife's casket. His audience—children, grandchildren, a smattering of friends—was captive.

"I just want to say that our minister is trained in church speak and church ritual. And he used a lot of words in today's service which might have been foreign to a lot of us. He spent a lot of time talking about Jesus Christ and the resurrection. I felt it was important to have a minister conduct this service. But let us remember the most important point from today's service: Patricia was an incredible person, a wonderful wife and mother, a loving grandmother. A great friend. Let's not have all that church speak get in the way of why we're here, why we gathered today: to celebrate her life, what an incredible person she was."

I turned and looked at the funeral directors who were standing near me and quietly asked, "So why in the hell did he invite me?"

One of the funeral directors quietly responded, "You should've been here when the family first came in for planning. Let's just say that when this family is out of our hair, we're going for drinks." We softly chuckled.

And I shouldn't have been surprised. A few days before the service one of his daughters had emailed me an order of service for the funeral. Perhaps she was unaware that clergy are trained and charged with arranging such matters. According to her outline the service would have lasted an hour and a half, included nine songs (all of which being "hits from the '60's and '70's"), five eulogists, and a couple of prayers fit for a church billboard.

What was missing from her order of service? Cut from the order of service were Bible readings, petition prayers, and a confession of faith. Also missing was music that referenced the God revealed in Jesus Christ. But she did leave me three minutes for a sermon. I had to negotiate for the presence of the Gospel in a funeral service I had been asked to lead. It felt like I was smuggling Jesus Christ into his own gig.

"Well, I guess a pastor would want it that way." Such was her response to my importing of Jesus Christ into the order of service.

When the service of committal at the cemetery was finished, I was asked if I wanted to go to dinner with the family.

"I'm honored. But no thank you." Not only had my presence made the family feel fifty shades of uncomfortable, but I had never felt more like a fifth-wheel in my life. It was time to go. Could this be—I have often asked myself—where solidarity with Jesus Christ begins in the ministry?

I never saw him again. Nor did I again see his lady friend who was a member of our congregation. He had sequestered her worship life into a community church in the next town over. I'm guessing that he had found in that congregation a God more agreeable. But, as time wore on, I did learn more about him through a church member who worked with him. Though such words could be considered gossip, I consider them pastoral insight.

I had learned that his wife had left him because he was abusive, both verbally and physically. I had learned that his social circle had now, essentially, consisted of him and his new lady friend. I had learned that his coworkers avoided him due to his temper. I had learned that he had stopped drinking cold turkey a handful of years ago. He swapped it out for religion. Religion works well in the context of addiction transfer. When such a transfer—from booze to religion—has been conducted, it becomes easier to detect evidence of one's righteousness. And there is nothing that funds more fully, more fanatically, retributive desires than a righteousness which is so unambiguous, so visible.

I learned that the daughter was a business professional with a rising career. She was able to merit—literally merit—her father's affection. Her commitment—to work, to achievement, to appearances—dovetailed with her father's standards. And honored him well.

The son was an altogether different matter. I learned that he was a cauldron of addiction and criminal behavior. He had dropped out of high school, leaving home at sixteen or seventeen after a physical altercation with his father. He had been incarcerated multiple times. He had served in both the county and state prison systems.

Not only did the son's addiction appear to reflect that of the father's, but—more importantly—it encroached upon his father's professional image. It tarnished the father's perceived image in the community. Whether or not the father felt responsible—for whatever reason—for the son's addiction and behavior I don't know. But certainly, the son was responsible for the father's image, and ultimately his honor. Satisfaction was due the father.

Perhaps his logic was as such: "Crucify the one who has crucified your own image." That advice column by "Reverend" must have been like soul balm for the father. And what better reinforcement of such an attitude than Christian doctrine (at least a caricature of one), specifically, atonement theory *à la* Anselm of Canterbury? Anselm of Canterbury's atonement theory, when pulled from its historical and theological context, can have cruel consequences when considered from the perspective of pastoral ministry.

I never had the opportunity to minister to this father. Nor, had he been a member of the congregation I was serving, would he have permitted me. Eventually he found a church whose teachings corresponded with his attitude. It is a frightful thought that Jesus Christ, his person and work, can be a wax nose shaped by dysfunction and the logic of retribution.

But this father, his outburst—and what I ultimately came to learn of him and his family—has always been a reminder that pastoral theology is the frontline filter, the litmus test, by which all theology is to be measured and evaluated. In this case, with respect to judging the validity of any atonement theory, might it be as simple as asking: Does it reflect the Father's life-giving commitment of love in Jesus Christ? Or is it merely a reflection of our sin, our estrangement from the love of God? Is it a reflection of God's crazy mercy? Or the world's bondage to retribution and violence? We can worship an idol which validates our retributive desires. Or we can worship God who has completely absorbed and suffered our violence.

That barren fig tree was not cut down on account of its barrenness. "Let it be," asserted the gardener to the vineyard owner. That barren fig tree became the responsibility of Jesus Christ. The barren fig tree's future became bound up with Jesus' life. So are those of the father and his son whose story I have briefly sketched.

God's honor, as Jesus Christ reveals, is not grounded in the restoration of God's personal image, but in the love by which that image is communicated to a humanity estranged from it. The logic of the former results in retribution. The logic of the latter results in mercy.

"Too much goddamn grace!" It almost sounds like evil's initial response to the rite of exorcism. Perhaps such a response should be the goal of a sermon informed by the ministry of Jesus Christ.

(6)

Ministry Boundaries

Blinded by our own Goodness

"There's been a hiccup." The bishop's assistant had called to update me regarding the call process. It is that period in which both congregation and pastor discern whether or not they are a good fit for one another.

It had been a month since I had heard anything from either the synod office or the congregation's call committee. And now I was learning the *why*. The call committee had gone rogue and was seeking—behind the backs of the congregation and the synod staff—interviews with pastor candidates outside of our church body.

"You can also use the format of a Bible study." During the call process I was given the option of presenting a short Bible study to the congregation or leading a worship service. I chose the Bible study. My rationale was that a Bible study would provide a better context for getting a glimpse of my personality and leadership style. It would include discussion which would facilitate dialogue.

The topic of the Bible study was Luke 10:25–37, famously known as the "Parable of the Good Samaritan." Although the book you hold in your hands is *not* a Bible study, I will briefly develop its substance. Here it goes . . .

+ + + + + + +

A man was traveling from Jerusalem to Jericho. He was beaten, stripped naked, and left for dead. The first one to arrive upon this man who "appeared dead"[1] was a priest. Should not his religious identity translate itself into a demonstration of mercy, of healing? The priest passed by on the other side.

The next one to encounter this man who "appeared dead" was a Levite. As with the priest, should we not expect from this man a demonstration of mercy, of healing? The Levite passed by on the other side. Enter the Samaritan.

But I won't call him *good*. Some background is required here.

He has entered stage left into a world ordered by racial purity. It was a society, according to a work published several decades ago,[2] classified by levels of purity. According to such a system of classification, the priest and the Levite sat on the top rung of the ladder as expressions of pure ancestry. The second rung of Jewish society was comprised of Jews who, though they could lay claim to pure ancestry, were either engaged in contaminating trades (i.e., a tanner), or, for one reason or another—most likely through debt default—had become slaves. The third rung consisted of illegitimate Israelites (a demographic which consisted of Gentile slaves, temple slaves, children born out of wedlock, and eunuchs—among others). Residing on the lowest rung of this society were the Samaritans.

The Samaritan was considered, as we factor in the law's prohibitions, something of a poster child for impurity. The Samaritan was not only considered an expression of mixed ancestry and therefore racial impurity, but a practitioner of paganism. The Samaritan's religious universe was centered on Mt. Gerizim and not the temple in Jerusalem. Periodically Samaritans were implicated in acts of temple vandalism and desecration. What purity-committed, first century Jew would call a Samaritan *good*? Are we getting a sense that this parable is *not* intended to be read prescriptively, that it is *not* fundamentally intended as a guide for Christian conduct? Now, let us apply this context to a reading of the parable . . .

For both the priest and the Levite the man who "appeared dead" was nothing more than a threat to their status, be it even a temporary sidelining of status. The law prohibits the handling of corpses (see Num

---

1. The word *hēmithanē* is most often translated as "half dead." I have translated it as "appeared dead" in order to capture the context, namely, the appearance of one who is nearly dead, who is barely hanging on to life, to those who—as will be developed—see the world through the lens of "pure" and "impure." It is my sense that this translation best fits the context.

2. See Jeremias, *Jerusalem in the Time of Jesus*.

19:10b–13). Whether he's a dead-as-a-doornail corpse, or simply an unconscious, bloody mess, exposure to such a man carries the risk of incurring an impurity-penalty prescribed by the law. Such a penalty will consist of a time-out for repurification. The threat of contamination trumps any display of humanitarian concern. And let us note: it's not that the man who "appeared dead" is invisible. It is worse than this. He is visible, but only as a threat to purity. When our gaze is calibrated to our commitments, and our chief commitment is to the maintenance of purity, then appearances can paralyze our empathetic impulses. Such a value system strips our gaze of its humanizing tentacles.

At the apex of this society, where temple religion and societal status converge, the parable narrates an exsanguination of mercy necessitated by the priority given to the maintenance of purity-derived identities and boundaries. The human who has been deemed a contagion becomes a mere *it* to be dodged on purity's playing field. Enter the impure Samaritan.

Only the Samaritan *sees* the man who "appeared dead." The Samaritan, upon seeing the man who "appeared dead," was "moved in the guts" (*esplangnisthe*). Not only was his *seeing* the beginning of the healing process (the bandaging of wounds, treating them with oil and wine, transporting him to an inn, permitting a blank check for this stranger's needs), but scholars tell us that such viscerally motivated demonstrations of compassion ("being moved in the guts" / *splangchnizomai*) are attributed in the New Testament to *divine* revelations of love.

Perhaps now we understand? It takes one who has been declared impure to see the humanity of the impure. It takes one who has been dehumanized to see the humanity of one who has been dehumanized. Divine mercy, its demonstration, is attributed to one who is impure. The contagion has become the source of healing. The threat has become the source of life.

The parable is not fundamentally about a *good* Samaritan whose kindness is to be emulated. Viewed from within his social context, do we really aspire to become like this Samaritan? The parable, instead, describes the crazy, beyond-the-bounds manner by which divine mercy is revealed "apart from the law" (Rom 3:21). Messengers of divine mercy cannot be vetted with reference to such matters as lawlessness and impurity.

The parable is not about doing and emulating, but *seeing*. It is about constantly adjusting our sight to the perpetually unanticipated sources of God's mercy and healing. The parable is providing a lens by which to appreciate the unanticipated manner of divine compassion. Divine mercy cannot be tribally vetted as to its sources or monitored for the purity of its distributing agents. It has the potential to flow from both victims and victimizers, from oppressed and oppressors with equal volume and force.

Salvation begins with seeing. Better, salvation begins with being seen. It begins by being seen by those we have dehumanized for being impure; for being a threat. Salvation begins when we receive the humanizing mercy we have denied others. In the process our sight for humanity, our humanizing sight, is restored.

The Samaritans among us are the means by which we receive back our humanity. The chief symptom of such a *salvation* is a type of pareidolia on account of which—instead of seeing faces everywhere—one cannot help but see the image of God in all whom one encounters, friend and sworn enemy alike. May the Samaritans among us contaminate our purity-derived, tribal bodies with such a merciful vision malady.

+ + + + + + +

Such was my summation of the parable to the congregation which was gathered: First, God's is a crazy, lawless love. Second, the ministers of God's crazy, lawless love can't be contained by any category of purity. Jesus Christ alone is our competence for bearing his healing mercy. And then I opened the floor to conversation and questions. The fellowship hall was packed. All were intent on evaluating the pastoral candidate standing before them.

The first hand to shoot up was that of an older woman. She was in her early 70s. I came to learn that she was known for her outspoken lack of charm and her direct, often coarse, manner of communication. A lack of self-awareness seemed to intensify these attributes. I called on her. She introduced both herself and her husband. Her husband, who was seated to her right, was—it seemed—more silent than silent, more docile than docile. She offered a pleasantry or two. And then she asked: "Pastor, what does the Bible say about gays in the ministry?" She paused. And then she reframed her question: "Are you saying that you don't agree with what the Bible says about homosexuality?"

A feeling of hopelessness stole over me. Or was it dread? Or anger? And then I responded in language I was sure she would understand as a Lutheran: "I believe, teach, and preach that Jesus Christ alone is our salvation. We are justified by Christ alone. We are not justified by sexual orientation."

I paused. She shot me a look of confusion. And then I offered an answer framed by the Bible study: "There are no limits as to who can demonstrate God's mercy."

She waited impatiently for an answer.

But why had they been seeking candidates outside the church body? It was a symptom of something deeper. Much deeper.

You see, as far as church bodies go, I belong to a young one. It has been in existence, precisely, since January 1, 1988. I serve within a denomination whose growing pains have been very public. Since its creation it has been forced to wrestle with such significant matters as—among other things—church polity (essentially a debate over the nature of congregational authority), church communion (the nature of communion with other church bodies), church doctrine (how the individual is related to the Word of God), and church office (who is permitted to serve the office of Word and Sacrament). In this case, with this congregation, the problem swirled around the last of these issues. Specifically: homosexuality and the office of ministry. Simply (in the language of that woman I told you about, above): "is it right for the *gays* to be ordained?"

A vociferous faction within the congregation, anticipating the wider church body's vote—which would be conducted a few years later culminating in a churchwide vote in favor of the ordination of homosexuals—decided that the church body had become, in the words of one of its (then soon to be) ex-members, "too goddamned liberal and too godless." It was time to take the congregation to higher, safer ground. The best time to begin this venture was during the call process.

By the time the bishop's assistant had called me, the covered-up call process had been exposed, the bishop had been contacted, a congregational meeting and vote regarding its future in the church body had been conducted (culminating in a *yes* vote), and the dissenting contingent of families departed to form their own congregation. One more pure.

"There's been a hiccup," asserted the bishop's assistant, describing what I have just narrated. He added, "The storm clouds have passed, do you still want to interview?"

"Of course," I replied.

One wave of storm clouds had passed.

There may not be a phrase which raises more red flags. There isn't a phrase—in my experience—which is more self-righteously freighted. It is this: "*Love the sinner, hate the sin.*" Have we ever stopped to examine the assumptions lurking behind the words?

Let me be clear: were one to mean by this sentence that—having been "justified by Jesus Christ alone"—that one's life is a perpetual attempt to conform one's self to the image of God in whom they are created, I'm on board. No argument here. But often, I've observed, this is not what is meant. Such a phrase is more like disgust concealed in a pious coating.

Such a phrase is often spoken from the perspective of an underhanded inclusivity. It is a feigned expression of grace which implicitly asserts that—certainly regarding homosexuality—I can welcome you while expressing my disgust of you. It is a way of saying "you're welcome among us as a fellow sinner, albeit you express sin in a manner more revolting."

It is spoken by folks who confess—normally at the beginning of worship, Sunday after Sunday—that "we are in bondage to sin and cannot free ourselves" (or other, similar words). It is the confession that everything we think, everything we say, everything we do emanates from "one who is curved in on oneself" (*homo incurvatus in se*) and is locked in a battle of self-assertion against God. This sin is so inextricably enmeshed with the self that—as the Lutheran reformers asserted—resurrection is its only purification.[3]

The long and short of it: if sin is bound so closely to sinners that God promises a resurrection in order purify us of it, then how are we able to make—apparently so easily—such distinctions regarding each other? *That* the God revealed in Jesus Christ unconditionally loves and unilaterally redeems sinners is both the promise upon which the church is founded and the scandal of its existence. I am called to love sinners. I'm not aware of another option.

But why had so many families split from this congregation to start their own? During the years of my call after their hiccup such was the question that framed much of my work in that congregation.

Some of the folks who had remained in the congregation blamed the hiccup on a relatively recent of arrival of a small group of "charismatic" Christians. According to the "traditional" faction, the "charismatic" faction wanted to infuse the congregation with a renewed focus on family values, in addition to updating worship with an atmosphere of *praise*. And some of the folks who had remained blamed the hiccup on a thirst for power between two sizable family systems. And some of the folks who remained blamed

---

3. See "Epitome," 488–89.

the hiccup on "families who, when it came right down to it, simply didn't like each other from the get-go." Those who had left the congregation were univocal in their declaration that the church body to which the congregation belonged had become too progressive, and dangerously so.

Small town congregational splits are no easy thing. The families, in many cases, have worshiped together for generations. They are often neighbors connected by ancestry and marriage. A split in a rural congregation is a like divorce in which the spouses keep cohabitating.

But it always seemed to me that the reason for the split ran much deeper than a fear of the progressive tendencies of a church body. It seemed as if the issue of sexuality and the office of ministry was something more of a pretext to execute a long-awaited exit.

Those who had left accused their previous congregation's church body of "not vetting their pastoral candidates for perverts" (in the words of one of the elders). Did this mean that they had been served by a homosexual pastor? The assumption (obviously): homosexuality is a form of perversion. But I also learned that the congregation's recent record of pastorates—these were colleagues whom I knew—didn't support such a case.

But even some of the old timers who remained with the congregation accused the church body to which this congregation belonged of not only "not vetting their pastoral candidates for perverts," but "not holding them accountable for their actions."

He was in his late-80s at the time. An old veteran. He had seen a lot of death and destruction in western Europe during World War II. There was a time early in my ministry in which many of my parishioners shared this experience. They are gone now. I miss them. This old vet liked his beer and wine. He liked his cigarettes. He loved his humanity. And he yearned for his wife.

By the time I knew him he had been a widower for many years. Though he came to worship regularly, I still visited him monthly. Visitation is primarily for the homebound, to keep them connected to the body of Christ. A pastor in a small community will make hundreds of visits over the course of their call's duration. His was a visit—retrospectively—I made for me.

During those visits we would enjoy a glass of beer. Perhaps a glass of red wine. In the summer, if it was hot, he would offer a glass of chardonnay with an ice cube. We would sip our drinks. And talk.

You knew you had been invited into a sacred place when he spoke of his military service in the Second World War, the day-to-day tedium, the carnage, the camaraderie which sustained him.

Prompted by a question I had asked about his wife, he once invited me into his "holiest of holies," that place where yearning love dissolved time, and memories played as if they were first-runs. He replied: "It's those cherry red lips, pastor, that I miss. And, by God, that hair, as gold as corn tassel, as soft." His eyes closed. And then he continued, "And those legs, with those black stockings she wore. I loved watchin' her prepare for a night on the town the together. And anticipatin' comin' home with her."

I listened intently. His yearning for his wife's intimacy was palpable.

He added, "I miss her warmth and her touch. A man's never too old to enjoy such love. She'd just stand there in the doorway. And I'd just stare. You can't imagine, pastor, how much I enjoyed her. And then she'd want to make love to me. To me." He paused. "She's been gone all these years, and I still fantasize about her touch, dream of her warmth. We shared quite a life together." Then he added, "By God, pastor, we'd better get our bodies in heaven. I'm gonna use mine to make love to her again."

Then he looked up, opened his eyes, took a sip from his beer—a moist track lined down his face—and simply said, "Pastor, I'm sensing it's not that far away." It wasn't. He added, "Makin' love to my woman again isn't an unchristian thing to pray for, is it?"

It's hard to imagine the new creation bereft of physical intimacy. It's hard to imagine heaven without all the entitlements of embodiment. I learned as much about Christian hope from him as I have from anyone. It is an embodied hope. I find it difficult to yearn for a future with God apart from these bodies which God declared "very good" from the very beginning.

Before I departed, I prayed for his *heaven*. Our *heaven*.

We confess "the resurrection of the *body*." I can't imagine bodies—before or after the resurrection—which don't require for their wholeness the touch, the warmth, the love, of the other.

"Pastor," she said over the phone, *"I know you're busy packing, but I need to talk."* Her voice was propelled by urgency. We scheduled a coffee visit for the next day at her home. She was in her late 70s and had been widowed for some time. She was an elegant woman. She never left her home without being gussied-up.

That next day we sat at her kitchen table exchanging pleasantries for a bit. We spoke of the past, of my time serving the congregation, of my imminent departure for another call. Then it got quiet. A pregnant, heavy pause fell over the room.

"I know you've been curious about what caused the split before you arrived here." She stopped. Then she continued, "I'm not trained in dealing with such matters as you are. I don't see the things that you see. I can only speak of what I know, of what I can confirm. And I think there is something you need to know." Her information came from an involved party. For the next stretch of time she took me into one of the darkest realms I've ever entered in ministry.

Before continuing with what she had to tell me, she looked to her left. Then to her right. It was as if she was scanning her home for spies. Her countenance dropped. Her voice lowered, hushed in such a manner that it appeared even a mention of the subject would land her in a gulag. Or, perhaps, such sharing would exclude her from the life of the congregation. She was scared yet impelled to speak. She opened-up about an era in her congregation's life.

Her knowledge came from a close, older female relative of hers, a widow. Her relative, she said, "had to get it off her chest." It was a story of profound boundary violations. It was a story of predation upon vulnerability. *Heterosexual* in nature. Over time it became a story of shame and resentment. Eventually it became a story of both congregational division and distrust for the wider church body to which the congregation belonged.

"Just as sure, pastor, as I'm sitting here," she said quietly, "did she [her older female relative] look me square in the eyes and tell me all of this." She continued, "I know it was embarrassing for her when I asked. She was old, nearing the end of her life. But I had to ask, partly to reconfirm it as true, partly because I couldn't believe this actually happened in my congregation." Again, she paused. She added, "Trust is what made that pastor so dangerous, I guess." As one who considers trust to be fundamental to Christian ministry, this last remark is horrifying.

A week later a separate source, an older gentleman, one who had served in congregational leadership at the time of the boundary violations, confirmed the events from another perspective. He spoke of multiple boundary violations. And yes, I was told, the leadership of the larger church body to which the congregation belonged was aware. This old congregational leader had witnessed a confession of the violations to the "head guy in the main [synod] office."

In retrospect, it seems that my imminent departure had opened the gates of communication. The prospect of my exit created the sense that I could be entrusted with a confession that was guaranteed not to jeopardize those who had confided in me. Perhaps it was the age of the confidants, combined with my imminent departure, that created a sense of "now or never" about sharing what they knew.

I sensed that the whole matter had been swept under the rug. Maybe that was *modus operandi* of the time. Future leaders were led to believe that churchwide discussions over the ordination of homosexuals was the reason for the congregation's split. This was certainly part of the issue. Fundamentally though, the split was something of an off-ramp from a relationship drained of trust surrounding a mishandling of sexual boundary violations, ones which were *heterosexual* in nature. Wounds which had been wrapped in silence festered and engulfed the congregation. Depending upon how they are managed, such wounds can either become the seedbed of healing, or the matrix in which resentment infinitely blooms. The wider church body became the target of resentment. Better, hostility.

I have spent much time thinking about the atmosphere surrounding, and created by, that congregation's hiccup. On the dissenting side—which eventually departed the congregation to start its own—churchwide conversations regarding homosexuality and the office of ministry provided a convenient exit from a relationship with the wider church body which had been dissolved of trust over the mishandling of sexual boundary violations. Violations which were *heterosexual* in nature.

But many of those who remained with the congregation simply chalked the exit up to bigotry, intolerance of *homosexuals* (which, certainly, was expressed by some who had exited). In the process, though, such a simplified explanation of the events only served—for many—to the magnify the collective goodness of the congregation and the church body to which it belonged. Essentially, if it weren't for such unambiguous expressions of bigotry, would our own goodness and virtue ever become so clearly *visible*? Do we ever appear as holy and righteous as when the evil around has become so clearly identified? Such an attitude, as I detected, created its own problematic. Let me briefly unpack this.

The desire for unambiguous visibility—of goodness, virtue, holiness, righteousness, etc.—requires the concealing of the violent vitalities which lurk at our core. Indeed, the very identity of such a position, to both define and sustain itself, *requires* an object of contempt. Yet we remain on the same spectrum as the object of our contempt, enlivened with the same spirit of animus and division. As such, we internalize the *modus operandi* of the very evil we have identified and targeted. Such a position reflects—with reference to the object of contempt (i.e., in this case the families who had exited)—not a difference in kind, but merely a difference in degree. In short, we become nothing more than a variation of the very evil we have claimed to abhor. We unwittingly ape the darkness we allegedly detest. Only now we view ourselves through the lens of *the holy*.

What is more, such is the logic and impulse which appears to inform various—not all—expressions of what is called *social justice*. *Social justice* is not synonymous with *Christ-justice*. And a clear distinction must always be made. We must always be clear whether it is Jesus Christ who is being served, or some other lord, one fed by a pound of flesh. *Social justice* is often only a difference in degree on the world's spectrum of retributive justice. *Christ-justice* is a difference in kind with reference to the former. Jesus Christ calls us to humanize—to see the humanity in—expressions of distorted humanity regardless of where—in whom—they may be encountered, in friend and foe, victim and victimizer, oppressed and oppressor alike.

Though it is tempting for the followers of Jesus Christ to plug themselves into the pulsating current of retribution for the sake of addressing the world's wrongs, in the process we become nothing more than another version of the world's animus and violence in the guise of the sacred. Only now it is holy retribution which promises that its expression of violence will be violence's final, magical form. Only to press the reset button on the world's cycle of violence.

Evil is never more destructive than when it has captivated its disciples to their core, animating their hearts and minds. That which we convinced ourselves was external and localized in the other now gushes forth from our hearts in holy packaging. How do we detect the evil which animates us, which has become the lens through which we see others? How shall we describe the monster which has swallowed us?

I remember well a time. That is, I remember a time in which *they*—"the gays"—became a foil which prevented a congregation from mercifully probing its darkness and trauma, the wounds created from that darkness and trauma, and its complicity in magnifying that trauma's effects. Many were lured into perpetuating holy hatred in the name of addressing hatred. Such a foil blinded them from naming and owning the darkness—and wounds created by that darkness—abiding at the core of their body.

To execute its intentions, evil requires a host body, one with which it is inextricably intimate. And so, it becomes a contamination only the resurrection can purify. The Lutheran reformers called it the purification of the resurrection. The promise of such a purification, ultimately, is that it will bring to *visibility* the image in whom we have been created. For now, that image—the image of God—is concealed, perceived only by the eyes of faith. For now, in light of the new creation, it is a contamination which is managed with self-awareness, repentance, and humility. Come, Holy Spirit.

(7)

Burying Babies

*Shepherding through Death
while Celebrating Life*

The father had just placed his newborn child in the ground. It was now my turn to stand in the grave with the deceased child. I had to speak the words of the burial liturgy. Their baby died from Sudden Infant Death Syndrome (SIDS). He was two-months-old at the time.

The father of the deceased baby had suggested that it would be best for me to stand *here*. The infant's grave had accidently been dug too wide. It was twice as wide as it needed to be. The extra space, as it had permitted the father to stand in his son's grave to manually lower his son's casket, also permitted me to stand next to the casket. Strangely, I can't remember how deep in the earth I stood. And I can't conjure a burial vault. Emotions play strange games with memory. The most obscure of details become salient. Things which should be obvious become blurred. Yet, the memory of this occasion is one I still feel in my guts.

Looking skyward from the hole, the mother's face—a canvas which seemed to alternate with grief and anger—emerged. Her grief had transfigured her countenance with an austere, pallid radiance. It seemed like her emotional upheaval was causing her to become transparent to the divine. Her face emitted a terrifying, sacred glow. That hole seemed bottomless.

Oh, and there was one more matter that shaped my awareness that day. We had just celebrated the birth of my daughter one week prior.

She was born in early June. Though a thunderstorm would roll through later in the evening, my daughter was born on a warm, beautiful Midwestern day. The sun's rays were refracted through various shades of green from the trees which rose up and greeted us in the second-floor hospital room in which we had welcomed our daughter.

Our son—the first of our two children—was born on the plains, in south-central Nebraska. He is our *Nebraska baby*. Our daughter was born in Iowa, in a Missouri River town. She is our *Iowa baby*.

Between the two children is a third child. It is a boy. For whatever reasons the pregnancy was a self-terminating one. One of the hard facts of the world is that it will crucify us. The human body is an expression of that world. What causes the womb to turn from temple of life to chamber of death is a mystery.

He was removed from my wife's womb at 19 weeks by means of a D and C (Dilation and Curettage). Regarding the process of his extraction: I have often sensed that the practice of medicine assumes it can conceal *gruesome* with such clinical terms as *procedure* and *comfort*. No level of technology or palliative-speak can beguile me from understanding the horror which often parades at the center.

I realized a couple of years ago that there was an extended period—beginning on the day we were informed of the dead child in my wife's womb and continuing for a duration of what appears to be ten to eleven weeks—of which I have no memory. I see the calendar dates for that period. I even attended a family wedding during that time. We have photos to prove it. My work calendar from that period indicated that I was busy doing ministry. But I can't recollect the contents of those days. It appears that I was physically but not psychically present.

What is interesting (and there is no resentment on this matter, it's just an observation) is that, though many in the congregation I was serving knew of my wife's pregnancy—for they had caught wind of it somewhere around its twelfth week or so—none responded to the termination of the pregnancy. We were too filled with grief to speak about it. And the congregation may not have known how to enter into the grief of its pastor and his family. I do remember a sense of alienation which had intensified my grief.

Over time the feelings of horror and grief have lessened in intensity. In their diminishment hope has arisen. We dream of him. We yearn to see him. To the point: my daughter's birth was framed by a newly acquired sense of life's fragility. Her life was sown and cultivated in the dark, rich soil of loss and grief.

I can't recall the genetic malady. And the specifics of the situation have been rounded off with the passage of years. But what I do remember is this: the couple's newborn child—a baby boy with thick tufts of brown hair—had only a matter of hours, perhaps a few at most, to live post-delivery.

The couple did not belong to the congregation I was serving at the time. The father's father—the grandfather-to-be—was a member of the congregation I was serving. The grandfather-to-be had wandered into my office several weeks prior to the delivery to inform me of the situation. He also made a request.

"Pastor," he asked, speaking in the tone of one holding back a wave of grief, "we would be much obliged were you to come to the hospital and baptize the child before he passes on."

"Absolutely," I responded.

At some point prior to the birthdate, the timeline of which I never learned, the doctors had informed the couple of the child's predicament. Yes, upon birth, at first, the child would appear healthy. But due to insufficient organ development, among other things, the baby's vitality would gradually slip away. The gift of each moment of life was also the slippage of another grain of sand through the hour glass. They would be able to hold him, love him, kiss him, caress him, coo to him. And then give the child back to God.

A window for the delivery had been given. I made sure that my schedule was flexible enough to facilitate my presence and the rite I was to conduct. The hospital was a twenty-minute drive from our residence. The grandfather-to-be would contact me when the mother was admitted to the hospital. And then when the delivery had occurred. The former call gave me something of a window of preparation while the latter call initiated my drive to the hospital.

Eventually the call came from the grandfather. And then the second call. And quickly I was on my way to the hospital with my handbook containing the "Rite of Holy Baptism." I was wearing a black clerical shirt, khaki pants, and a black blazer. I would eventually leave the blazer in the car.

Arriving at the hospital, I quickly made my way to the neonatal unit. The nurses, knowing I would be coming, buzzed me into the unit and gave me the room number. I arrived at the bedside of a mother holding her newborn child surrounded by the father and two sets of grandparents.

Due to the adversities in which they minister, pastors are often called into sacred, intimate spaces with complete strangers with little segue. Which means: trust is often cultivated more with countenance and body language than it is with words. Too few words seldom make trust building more difficult. The same can't be said for too many words. Also, as the couple and one set of grandparents lived some distance from the community in which I was serving, my warm relationship with the other set of grandparents created an atmosphere receptive to my presence.

With each exhale the baby's life was slowly ebbing away.

He was wrapped in a soft, white nursery blanket. And then wrapped by his mother's arms. Any form of distress that I may have anticipated was missing from the baby boy's face. His countenance had the appearance of pure contentment. Cradled in his mother's arms, he was in the safest place in the universe. Yet the specter of death was inscribed into every second of the scene.

Eventually—taking my cue from the grandfather I knew—I initiated the "Rite of Holy Baptism." At our request one of the nurses had brought in a bowl of lukewarm water. The water doubled as the liquid by which the sign of the cross was made on the baby boy's forehead following the Baptism.

"I baptize you in the name of the Father, and of the Son, and of the Holy Spirit."

Gently water was applied to the baby boy's head three times.

Gently his head was tamped with the baptismal cloth when the Baptism was completed.

"Child of God, you have sealed by the Holy Spirit and marked with the cross of Christ forever."

Gently the sign of the cross was made above his eyes.

Gently, deeply the baptismal party wept.

Eventually I departed that sanctuary.

The grandfather called me a couple of hours later. The newborn baby boy died about an hour and a half after I departed their company. Until his death, and following—as was relayed to me by the grandfather—he remained secure in his mother's arms.

The Baptism was conducted just over a month after we celebrated the birth of our daughter. Upon coming home from the conducting the Baptism I held my daughter in my arms.

My wife was pregnant again. Yet the news of her pregnancy didn't strike us with the unadulterated joy which the first two pregnancies did. This time the news of pregnancy created a mixture of joy and fear. The miscarriage of our second child, the D and C performed on my wife, was just months in the past. The joy of pregnancy was framed by the pain and grief of life and dreams crucified *in utero.*

If the first two pregnancies created a buzz of excitement, this third pregnancy was accompanied by an atmosphere of cautious sobriety. The experience of pain and grief has a way of causing the heart to become cautious, circumspect in its steps forward.

I'm pretty sure that we waited approximately until week 20+ to inform anybody of my wife's pregnancy. I'd like to tell you that superstition didn't play a role regarding the delay of communication regarding her pregnancy. But I'd be lying. This third pregnancy was enveloped completely by God. And whatever assistance God could use.

The cemetery was just about a mile outside of town. The funeral procession, I was told, would probably extend from the cemetery back into the town. By the time the hearse—in which I would be riding—reached the cemetery, the final cars in the procession would be pulling onto the highway and heading to the cemetery. Such a scenario meant, as I had calculated it, that I would be able to locate a pocket. I will return to that thought in a moment.

The funeral that day was for a two-year-old boy. He had been born with a heart defect. During his short life, from within days after his birth to within a couple months of his death, he had endured countless heart procedures. Apparently—either shortly before his birth or shortly after, I'm not sure which—the parents were told that, due to the nature of his heart defect, his birth was a death sentence. Corrective surgery after his birth would only prolong his life by months, a year at best.

I don't recall very many details about the parents. But I do remember that they were young, perhaps in their early-20s. And I do remember the love that bonded them. And I vividly recall how they embraced each other while standing in front of their child's open casket. I remember seeing a love so palpable that it seemed to connect the living with the dead. I remember seeing a little boy, though lying in in a casket, who seemed ready for a family photo after a short nap. Certainly not a one-way trip to the cemetery.

The funeral was packed. The sanctuary was standing room only. The glass double doors at the back of the sanctuary had been opened for overflow extending into the fellowship hall. The young parents, flanked by their parents, sat in the first pew, just in front of the pulpit. I still see their faces.

The assembly that gathered around the parents that day was a sprawling, living, breathing, heaving body whose energy melded into a current which ebbed and flowed with the readings, the hymns, the message, the prayers, the benediction. The sanctuary felt as if it was a ship tilting back and forth on an open sea of grief. Now this way, now that way. "Hold on," I remember thinking to myself while leading the service, "we will be delivered." *To what*, or *For what* . . . I hadn't articulated to myself.

Ultimately the service was completed. And we filed out to the waiting vehicles for the funeral procession to the cemetery. I was directed to the hearse at the front of the line where I would ride shotgun. And it was here, sitting alone in the hearse while the funeral director was organizing the funeral procession, that the reality I had been keeping at bay came flooding in.

I had time to reflect on death. The death of a child. The death of parents' dreams. Such reflections, naturally, were framed by the birth of our daughter just months prior. And the loss of our son *in utero* before that. This pause between the funeral service and rite of committal ushered into awareness thoughts and emotions I had been keeping at bay to perform my duties as a pastor. Aware of my own emotional involvement, I had attempted to bracket my emotions so that I could be present with the family in theirs. I wanted to demonstrate solidarity. I wanted to project stability and assurance and comfort. But I also wanted to lead the funeral service without becoming overwhelmed by it. Which meant: I had not cried. I needed to cry. And, though he was my good friend, not in front of the funeral director, either. I needed to cry. Yet I did not want to be seen crying.

So, as I calculated it (based upon what I had been told about the nature of the procession): if the hearse would be the first vehicle to arrive at the cemetery, and the hearse would be followed by a long procession extending down the highway (which would take several minutes to coordinate and park), then I would have an interval of time to vacate the hearse and—certainly with my back turned to the procession pulling up—*investigate* the grave site. This would be my pocket. To cry.

And so, it occurred as I had envisioned it. The procession pulled out onto the highway. And, a mile down the highway, we pulled into the cemetery. And, pulling into the cemetery, the hearse rolled up to the grave site. The funeral director got out and assisted in coordinating the procession which was pulling in. And then I seized the moment. I walked around the front of hearse to *investigate* the grave site. My back was turned to the procession pulling in. My posture looked poised and professional.

Then, for about a minute, I wept quietly, yet violently, deeply. It was managed heaving. Wiping my eyes and cheeks with my jacket sleeve, I turned to continue my duties as a pastor. A service of committal for a two-year-old boy beckoned.

As the father of a newly born daughter, just months old on this day, I was called to bury a beautiful two-year-old boy, to accompany and comfort his parents through the very horror and grief that had infiltrated my deepest parts.

It wasn't a lesson I learned in seminary. I don't know how one would even teach such a lesson in that context. Such a lesson requires the classroom of life. And such lessons have more to do with wisdom than knowledge. The attainment of such wisdom can only be suffered.

That lesson is this: the vocation of pastor is not an insulated one. It is not a vocation which is isolated from others (whatever they may be). It is not as if somehow one could—in a compartmentalized fashion—flip a switch to become a pastor in this moment, a parent in the next, a son or neighbor after that. It is not an attitude or mentality which flips on with the beginning of a rite, only to flip off after the benediction has been spoken. It is a vocation in which all others converge and coalesce to inform the compassion which animates the ministry of Jesus Christ.

Which means: the vocation of pastor isn't simply informed by the spectrum of life's vocations and experiences. The vocation of pastor is also informed by an understanding of what can occur when one *fails* to acknowledge one's immersion in the spectrum of life's vocations and experiences with those they serve. The pastor, too, experiences a life whose spectrum spans from the depth of loss and grief to the joy of welcoming new life. And everything in between. To push from awareness that spectrum may well eliminate the empathy which informs how the ministry of Jesus Christ can be conducted; which connects a pastor with those she serves.

In the birth of our daughter, one occurring in a context of loss and grief, arose not simply a hallelujah to new life, but a hallelujah enriched with an empathy born of that same loss and grief. It was an empathy which was able to see and understand, which was able to love and serve, that loss and grief in the lives of others. The birth of our child in our valley of the shadow of death informed how I was shepherding this young couple through theirs.

A broken hallelujah always bears the promise of being a healing hallelujah.

(8)

Ministering from Grief

A Special Grief

"Get over it," the old man said. "We all lose family." And then, executing any attempt to interpret his words charitably, he finished, "Your grief isn't any more special than mine."

"Good day," he said, turning and walking away from my office door.

My heart had already been wounded that fall. Now it felt torn in two. The *coup de grâce* been had been delivered by an elderly man who was recognized as one of the pillars of the congregation.

Oh, the ease, the matter-of-factness, the economy of words, by which it was expressed. It still leaves a shiver down my spine. I sat there behind my desk—I had been preparing the weekly prayers for Sunday worship—paralyzed. First by disbelief. Next by confusion. Finally, by anger. Who needs enemies when such a personality is in your flock? I went for a walk to clear my mind.

It was the last thing on my mind while preparing for ministry. I threw myself into biblical Greek and Hebrew. I learned the fundamentals of biblical exegesis and preaching. I drank deeply from the well of my tradition's theology. I took courses in worship and pastoral care. I began to articulate theology in my own voice.

I envisioned the time in which I would be officiating worship. I imagined the ecumenical ventures I would be facilitating with other congregations in the communities to which I would be called. I wondered about the nature of the crises through which I would be shepherding God's people. I envisioned the type of servant-leader I would be.

But it never crossed my mind that there would come a time that I would be ministering to grief while wading in my own. I had never considered the prospect that I would be healing hearts while carrying around a broken one. The diagnosis of my father's cancer (a myxofibrosarcoma which originated in his upper arm), his subsequent illness and death, was one such occasion.

+ + + + + + +

His forebears were known for their longevity. Indeed, both of his parents—my grandparents—died in their early 90s. As well, my father was a medical doctor. He had been trained in recognizing symptoms of illness. How did his own slip past his detection? Having factored in both his family's track record of longevity and his encyclopedic medical knowledge, I assumed that only old age would take him from this life. At the time of the diagnosis, he was seventy-years-old. I don't consider that old.

He was both my father and my confidant. He was the person I went to for advice and perspective. I learned a theology of pastoral care in seminary. I learned how to apply it as a human being to other human beings from him. He taught me that listening has as much to do with the eyes and feeling one's way into people than it does with the ears. He modeled the reality that no human being is beneath me.

Dad cast a critical eye to expressions of religion which placed the institution before the message. And had no stomach for dogmatism in any field. He never considered himself to be *religious* in any conventional sense of the term. I'm pretty sure that if *salvation* was a term in his lexicon, it had more to do with becoming human and recognizing, serving that humanity in others. Whatever *salvation* entailed for him, I'm certain that it revolved around embodied humans in this world.

+ + + + + + +

Dad called me the day he received his diagnosis. "Son, I've got cancer." He continued—almost sounding as if he was a doctor talking about another patient—by naming the cancer and breaking down its pathology. And then he said, "If I don't go through treatment, I have four to five months. If I go through treatment we're looking at something like a year. It's got its hooks into me. I reckon I've got a struggle in front of me." Nothing in his voice signaled despair or fear. At the middle of the storm was the same, soothing tone with which he had always reached into me. When the call was finished, I wept from the depths. I cried a cry that left me gasping for air. To breathe felt like a conscious decision.

My father would live nine months from diagnosis to death. During that time my understanding of God's omnipotence evolved. Any remnants of *Jesus as miracle worker* was eventually scrubbed clean from my mind and heart. I absorbed into my marrow the truth that the God revealed in Jesus Christ is not a *deus ex machina,* or a god which swoops in to turn around hopeless situations. Such a god—a *deus ex machina*—simply reacts on the terms which death sets. The God revealed in Jesus Christ makes of death a sacrament, a sign, of God's life-giving Lordship. Prayer grounded in such a God understands that death is not avoided, but harnessed to serving new creation. "Thy will be done" is an expression of a petitioner who has been crucified of agency to perceive, be animated by, God's life-giving agency concealed in suffering and death. My hope had been purified of optimism. All loopholes of immortality by which one would conceive of continuity through death were obliterated. God alone became my—and my father's—future.

Though I grieved intensely during those months of his illness, I came to understand more profoundly the Christ hope I had been proclaiming in my own ministry: complete new creation from old creation. Until that point hope had only been an idea. Now the promise of new creation no longer circumnavigated complete death. Everything went through it. Jesus was finally the crucified God. And this God was finally the Creator.

Ministry didn't stop because I was grieving. And there were times both during my father's dying process and after his death in which I wanted to stop amid the demands and deadlines of ministry and declare, "I'm grieving, can't you see? Why can't somebody pray for me, on my behalf?"

I came to learn that a pastor's grief can create an awkward tension among those whom a pastor ministers. Though I learned to mute my grief, when it did reveal itself, it was clear that it made many parishioners uncomfortable. A crack in the pastor's armor of sanguinity can be discombobulating in an atmosphere which desires pious, moral platitudes and praise music. Perhaps that old man's words—so cold, so indifferent, so cutting—were grounded in his discomfort at the prospect of grief clinging so tightly to a person who was called to be upbeat and optimistic.

Regardless, I was called to serve that old man. He was an old, Lutheran pietist. He was a veteran. I was told that he was quite a green thumb, a real nurturer of plants and flowers. Demonstrating compassion for vegetation is less demanding than demonstrating it among other humans. He has always served as a sober reminder that *piety* and *Christian love* are not synonymous terms.

Week after week I pushed forward. As my father was dying, I continued to go about my list of visitations. I continued my biblical exegesis and sermon preparation. I continued my Bible studies. I conducted the scheduled meetings. Week after week I continued to make home and hospital visits. I shepherded families through dying and death. And I conducted funerals.

Once my father's death had occurred and he had been buried my week of bereavement leave was up. It was as if—on schedule—I was to continue conducting ministry as if nothing had happened. It was as if my wounds were officially recognized as healed. From that point forward nothing more was said about the matter.

But I learned that grief's healing is not linear. Instead, it is something like a long cycle of stages in which any one stage can overlap with another. I found myself shepherding families through terminal diagnoses and stages of dying which were triggering my own grief. It seemed at times that I was ministering to grief from a bottomless pit of grief; proclaiming the promise of the resurrection from the valley of dry bones. In retrospect, some pretty good sermons—my opinion alone—came from this period. Nothing mechanical. Nothing dogmatically contrived. Something new was cultivated in me by preaching the Christ hope from such a location. That *something* was the *wisdom* that was finally accompanying my *knowledge* of the Word. I came to embrace this as a privileged perspective of *faith*.

But another issue arose in the context of ministering from my grief. It is one of which I must always be aware. Having lost both of my parents by maladies that came out of left-field before I turned forty, I must always be on guard in my ministry for resentment. I must always be vigilant of a lurking resentment for folks who have had twenty-plus more years to spend with their parents; folks whose parents die in their late-80s and 90s. There is always that voice—when ministering to such folks upon the death of their parents—that initially wants to say, "Why are you so sad? Look at all this time you had with them. Why aren't you celebrating their long life? Why are you grieving so intensely? Why aren't you grateful for all the time you had with them?" When called-out, such sentiments quickly recede.

And I have also come to understand that grief has two trajectories. Left unaddressed, left unexposed to a healing process, it evolves into a suspended state of resentment whose slogans are "Now you know how I feel!" and "Did you think you were special?" When hearing about tragedy its response is often one of *Schadenfreude*.

I was pastor to a woman who had tragically lost a child at a young age. Each time there was a tragedy in the community involving someone on the younger end of the spectrum, she would be one of the first in the community to reach out to the grieving family. On the surface such acts of ministry were beautiful. But the alacrity of her response never quite seemed right.

She confirmed my suspicions one day when I thanked her for her ministry. To my response of gratitude for her ministry she simply replied, her brow furled and her eyes glazed with coldness, "Now they *know* how I feel."

I shuddered. Grief had hardened into resentment seeking solidarity.

It is my experience that when grief is addressed, when healing begins to occur, a new manner of hearing and seeing begins. In the healing of grief is cultivated an empathetic vigilance which can see and feel its way into the wounds of others. In our grief, its healing, lurks the potential for our Christ-seeing. I have come to understand that my grief, its healing, bears within it the promise of one of my greatest assets as a minister: empathetic understanding and its ability see, to humanize, those whom I serve. Left unaddressed and unhealed, it becomes an interminable resentment. Resentment becomes a monster whose hunger for victims is never satisfied.

"Your grief isn't any more special than mine." The old man's words sliced my heart open like a scalpel. They were placed with a precision that almost seemed rehearsed. Yet such words may not have been intended to inflict harm. Perhaps they were an expression of a callousness forged by a long-practiced habit of self-protection.

Regardless, I have sat with his words over the years. I have let them sink into the deepest part of me. I have meditated with his words as if they were prayer beads. I have prayed within them. And because of that I must disagree with his declaration. But it isn't a self-justifying disagreement, or even one issued from malice.

Though he died long ago, what follows is the disagreement I would speak to him given the chance: "Yes, dear old friend, my grief is special.

That is, after a long, arduous process of healing I have come to understand how my grief can become, has become, a source of my ability to see and serve your wounds, your grief, as your pastor. Such is the promise of my grief, of what makes it special."

Within the healing of grief stirs the gift of discernment. It is a gift which has freed me to stand amid a spectrum of wounds with the ability to see and serve those whose crucified image I share. It is revealed by a gaze which peers through the cracks of cruciformity to conduct the ministry of Christ's love and understand its promise of healing.

Nobody invites grief. It is a symptom of hearts and relationships ripped apart. Yet it bears, with time and proper cultivation—when fractures and wounds become the soil of healing—the promise of becoming gift. It is a gift which should not be wasted within the ministry of Jesus Christ. To do so comes at the cost of seeing and hearing the wounds of those around us, the ones we are called to serve.

(9)

Risking Friendship

Saying Goodbye while Saying Goodbye

"**Don't make close friends within the congregation,**" asserted my elderly colleague. He was ordained in the 1950's. I was ordained almost fifty years later. The advice was logical. Healthy ministry requires the maintenance of healthy boundaries. Healthy boundaries also reduce the chance that one is accused of playing favorites. Healthy boundaries diminish the possibility of double binds, or relationships which send conflicting messages regarding a pastor's role and authority.

But such advice also assumes the pastor (along with his/her family) is not an embodied, sentient being who is sustained by—like those the pastor is called to serve—*relationships*. Such advice assumes that the pastor will be sustained by relationships outside the community in which they have been called to serve and invest themselves. Such advice assumes that pastors are unlike those to whom they are called to minister in that, namely, they won't "hit it off" with certain personalities and families experiencing similar stages in life.

We became close friends.

She came from a large family with many siblings. Outgoing. Intelligent. Earthy. Funny as hell. Although she was a beautician when we first met, she may well have made for a better lawyer with her sharp mind and global thinking. Her sense of perspective was broad.

He hailed from a smaller family, one with deep roots in the community. Though less extroverted than his wife, he too was intelligent, yet in more of a bookish fashion. He was a history buff. He worked the third shift as a member of maintenance personnel at a local factory in the next town over. Both were wildly devoted to their children.

We were at very similar stages in life. Our worldviews were similar. Our senses of humor were shared. Uncannily so. We connected. We developed a friendship. Our children were at the same stages of life. We were going through similar stages of parenthood. We watched their kids. They watched ours. We ate out together. Their friendship became lifeblood.

I saw him three different times that night. It was a clear, beautiful Monday evening in early fall and the town was brimming with activities. It seemed there were kids everywhere, either engaged in sports activities at the local park, or involved in church youth group activities. There was also a great deal of energy at the fire station where members of the fire department were conducting their monthly meeting/inspection. They were shining a newly acquired fire engine.

The first time I saw him that evening was on our doorstep. He had stopped by to ask whether we had seen his youngest son. The second time I saw him that evening was thirty minutes later. He was a few blocks away, in the southeast part of town. He had taken one of his children to a sports practice at the community park. We waved at each other. The third time I saw him was about an hour after that. We were heading to another town to get a bite to eat. It was around 7 p.m. This time he was sitting atop the fire department's newly acquired fire engine. He had donned a fire helmet and appeared to be cleaning the vehicle's exterior. We waved at each other. He was basking in the *esprit de corps* of the fire department.

His commitment to the volunteer fire department was followed by his work on the maintenance staff during the third shift at the bakery up the road. His shift, I believe, started at 11 p.m. It was a thirty-minute drive to work. His shift would finish at 7 a.m. Having arrived back at home, he would then take his two youngest boys to the elementary school where classes started at 9 a.m. After that he would sleep through the morning into early afternoon.

He had just turned 39 that summer. I was only two months behind him in age. As both of us were approaching 40 we used humor to balance our thoughts about getting older.

"I can't believe I survived my 39th birthday," he exclaimed that July. We laughed.

"Hey look," he said, "you have nothing to worry about. I came through it without a scratch."

For my 39th birthday he gave me a bottle of Dewars. I have not opened it.

"Pastor, are you standing?" It was 8:12 a.m. Having answered the parsonage phone, that was the question posed to me by one of my parishioners. He was a teacher. He was calling from the high school. Classes there started at 8 a.m. I had been standing in the parsonage kitchen drinking coffee. I was preparing for the day.

"What's up?" I responded.

He proceeded to tell me that Doug "was killed in car wreck just a mile outside of town." He explained, as he understood the report, that Doug was coming back from work and hit the back of a school bus that had stopped on the side of the highway to pick up kids.

I had to sit down. It felt as if the kitchen floor had dropped out from under me. My mind became a film loop of the previous night: Doug on our doorstep looking for his child. Doug at the community park with his son. Doug sitting on the top of the fire engine. Then his image flooded in: Doug's eyes. Doug's voice. Doug's humor. Doug's gentle demeanor. Doug the husband. Doug the father. Doug the son. Doug the sibling. Doug the friend.

He then added, "Doug's oldest son is here at the high school. He doesn't know what has happened yet. The counseling staff wants you, as his pastor, to come down and break the news."

"Sure," I responded. "How soon?"

"As soon as you can," he responded. "When you arrive, we'll pull him out of class and bring him down to the counseling office." Ultimately, they wanted me to then escort him home. His house was only three blocks away from the high school. It would seem like a mile.

"Give me fifteen minutes."

During those fifteen minutes, as I was preparing to head to the high school, I broke the news to my wife who had travelled to the closest city to get packing boxes from the grocery store. I almost forgot to mention: we were moving in five days. I had resigned my call after five years for another one.

The first thing out of my mouth to her, as if the initial manner of messaging had crystallized in me, was, "Are you sitting?" She asked why.

"Doug was killed this morning in a car wreck just outside of town," I said. The phone went silent. Then sobbing. And more sobbing. She was sitting.

"I need you to come home when you're ready to drive. Please don't drive until you're ready." Suddenly I didn't trust my wife's driving that morning. I always took it for granted before that morning.

He was a man of family and work. I can't count the times I asked Doug how he did it, namely, made time for his children's school events and sporting contests. Especially with his work schedule. His responses always reflected his love of being a father. "I can't imagine life without all this stuff."

The thirty-minute drive to and from work was travelled at night and during the early morning hours just around sunrise. It was often the case that Doug, having slept through the morning and early afternoon, would attend his children's school and sporting events before making the drive to work. I would pepper Doug with such questions as, "Where do you get all the energy?" "How much coffee do you drink?" "Are you really human?"

He knew what I was driving at. "I'm always rested and safe," he declared.

That morning school started at 9 a.m. for his two youngest kids. As always, their father was coming home from work. Young kids, fresh from a night of sleep, were awaiting their dad.

I was sitting in the high school's counseling office. School officials were retrieving Doug's oldest son from his first class of the day. My heart was racing.

The counseling office had a window on one side. It was the side facing the main office. I'm assuming that such a configuration permitted both verbal privacy and professional transparency. From the chair in which I was sitting, a black leather office chair with wheels on a four-pronged base, I could see the door through which school officials would escort Doug's oldest son. From this perch I quietly struggled with how to break the news to his son.

How does one communicate to a teenage boy that his father has been killed? What words should I use? What expression should my face wear (in addition to grief I can't seem to conceal)? Do I preface my message with a "Good morning"? Do I use the word *passed*? Do I use the word *died*? Do I use the word *killed*? Do I hug him? Do I give him space? As always, the situation dictated my actions.

He appeared in the window with a happy-go-lucky smile. Then he read my face. He observed the school officials who were around me. His steps became more cautious. He cracked the door slowly as if he was acclimating his eyes to the dark. He cautiously stepped inside the room. The door closed behind him. He paused.

"What's going on?" he asked. His wavering voice ascended several notes in his short question.

"Hey," I said, gently addressing him by name. "I need you to have a seat." I pointed to the chair which was directly in front of me about two feet from my knees. Haltingly, he made his way to the chair. Behind me, forming a crescent, stood members of the counseling staff. He sat.

"Pastor," he said, "what's wrong? Why are you here? Is everything alright? Please tell me everything's ok."

The message I had to communicate was both necessary and impossible. Though I had agonized over the choice of words to communicate his father's death, they gently slipped through my lips. "Your father was killed in a car wreck this morning while returning from work."

There was a brief, silent pause.

Then he drew back in the chair. "Mom, where's my mom?! Is she ok? I want to see my mom!" Without hint of coiled energy, he sprang from the chair. In one, seamless motion he was at the door. Somehow, I had managed to intercept him. I bearhugged him as gently as possible. I can still feel that hug. Embracing him, having placed my right hand on the back of his head, I simply said, "I'm going with you. You're not going alone." Together we walked the three blocks back to his home.

I've retraced Doug's final drive. To some such an exercise may seem morbid. For me it is a path of discovery and connection.

Beginning from the parking lot of his place of employment, I have attempted to perceive the final moments of life through his eyes. I have attempted to see what he saw. I have tried to feel what he felt. I have attempted to discern his state of mind. I have tried to grasp . . . him.

But there is an aspect of retracing his final journey of which I have become conscious: it is the thought, the wish, that such a ritual will conjure Doug from the dead. Or that, perhaps, such a ritual will channel another outcome. Maybe I will catch up to him and convince him to pull over for a breath of fresh air. Maybe he'll see me in his rear-view mirror. And then I will motion for him to pull over. Then disaster would be averted. I have entertained fantasies of somehow piloting him the final way home to his family.

I have approached the spot on the highway where the crash occurred and fantasized that it was a portal through which fantasy and reality's horror were flipped. Commensurate with such a fantasy, I have often conjured an unscathed Doug on the final stretch into town past the crash site. It is a Doug anticipating the day's events, reuniting with his kids, having a bite of breakfast, ferrying his two youngest to school. Grabbing a long nap. Enjoying the day with his wife.

Doug's grave overlooks the final approach to his location of death. When the cold, sober, indifferent evidence to its contrary is spying one's steps, keeping fantasy afloat is hard work.

"Is he showable?" That was my question to the town's funeral director. It came in response to a conversation I had with Doug's widow.

Doug left for work on Monday night. The crash occurred on Tuesday morning. On Wednesday Doug's widow pulled me aside while on a visit to their home. "Pastor," she said, "My son told me last night that this all feels like one big prank people are playing on us. I don't know what to say to him." She added, "He hasn't seen his father since Monday evening. He thinks it's all a prank. He needs closure."

"I need to think about this one." I knew about the nature of the crash.

I had seen the funeral director's vehicle parked in front of the funeral home only minutes earlier. Stepping outside, I glanced down the street toward the funeral home. His vehicle was still there. The funeral home was an old, two-story building which once served as a residence. Though I have never liked funeral homes, on the continuum of comfortability this one has always been one of my favorites. I left their home and walked down the street to the funeral home where Doug had been taken. The walk only took a few minutes. I encountered the funeral director on the porch just as he was making his way out for an errand. He invited me inside.

A brief conversation ensued. We went over the nuts and bolts regarding Doug's services, both his prayer service (the evening before his funeral, as was customary in that town), and his funeral service. Burial location was also clarified.

I then asked my pressing question, "Is he showable?"

There was a pause.

We were both aware of the nature of the trauma. As the funeral director he was intimately aware. As the pastor I was anecdotally aware.

Doug's compact car had slammed into the back of school bus stopped on the shoulder of the highway just a mile or so outside of town. It was estimated that he was traveling at the highway's speed limit when the collision occurred. There were no skid-marks leading up to the school bus. Whether children were in the process of boarding or had already boarded, I'm not sure. None were injured. In fact, reports from children who were on the bus indicated that the collision was only experienced as a "bump" with a muffled "boom."

The collision was not "bumper to bumper." Doug's hood slipped under the bumper of the bus suchwise that the windshield area of his car bore the brunt of the collision. Death was instant. My guess, and it's only a guess—although the absence of skid marks is telling—is that Doug had dozed off. As they say, "he never knew what happened."

Mentioning that I had just spoken to his widow, I indicated that "right now, one of her sons thinks it's all just a prank." I continued, "They need to see their father for the sake of closure, to say good-bye. Would we be able to arrange a private viewing, say, before the prayer service?"

The funeral director paused. His face was animated with sympathy.

"We can make it work," he responded. "I can't hide the damage, but I can make him presentable." He then explained how he would attach a veil from the casket lid to the casket sides. Such a veil permits viewing while diminishing the details of trauma, such as bruises, distortions, and lacerations. Upon approval from his widow, we were able to provide the family a private viewing prior to the general viewing which would was scheduled before the evening prayer service.

The decision to show Doug was one of the most difficult decisions in which I have ever been involved. Was I contributing to closure, facilitating a goodbye, or—due to the nature of his wounds—intensifying his family's trauma? I still see those children approaching their father's open casket. And then I have to stop thinking. I continue to pray—as I have regarding so many other occasions—that I made the right decision.

Doug's veil created an ethereal, dream-like quality about his appearance. When I see Doug in my dreams, though he is smiling and chatting, that veil is always present.

It would be one of my final official acts as a pastor to that congregation. It was a beautiful fall day. The sun ruled over a cloudless day. The air was cool. The leaves were beginning to turn colors. Fall's signs were everywhere in that farming community.

It was a mid-morning funeral. Traditionally folks were seated up until the minutes before the beginning of a funeral. In the case of Doug's funeral, the sanctuary was packed well before start time. The fellowship hall behind the sanctuary, to which it opened, was also packed. From the chancel it looked like an acre of people. Distraught people. People waiting for comfort.

Doug's widow, his three children, his parents and siblings, his grandparents, sat directly before the chancel in the first couple of pews. His widow and children occupied the first pew. I still see them clearly.

I see his widow. Yes, I just employed the word *his*. *Widow* is one of the few terms for which death does not dissolve, but indeed initiates, the field of the possessive pronoun. In life she was not *his* widow. Just *his*. And he *hers*.

She was in front of me, to the left. I wanted to hold her instead of preaching to her. Her children were to her left. They would come to more fully comprehend the implications of their father's death as they proceeded through the rites of manhood. Doug would have been a hell of a shepherd through that process. The discovery of death's implications is ceaseless in this life. It provides a painful surplus.

I have never revisited the sermon I preached that day. I will not. It is yesterday's bread. It has always been my prayer that, on the day of Doug's funeral, it was for his family a form of daily bread, a Word of promise which fed and sustained them. Like manna, a sermon cannot be hoarded. We must speak the promise anew each day.

Eventually we would bury Doug on a hill overlooking the last stretch of his life's journey. In the valley of the shadow of that hill is a tormented path of good bye. In the valley of the shadow that road will always seem like the final station of the cross.

"Don't make close friends within the congregation," asserted my elderly colleague. I completely understand that old fellow's point, its logic. Recognizing the mess that close friendships within a congregation can make—from double binds, conflicts of interest, to accusations of favoritism—I have always been vigilant (though not always successful of their maintenance) of such dynamics. I have served in the aftermath of calls in which the integrity of the office of pastor had been compromised by poor boundaries. But I also understand the needs of my humanity. I have come to understand that good friendships, especially the older I get, are a form of daily bread. They feed us, sustain us.

I did establish a close friendship within a congregation. I—along with my family—made close friends with Doug and his family. It was a friendship which sustained us. Me. Were I to know its outcome in advance, a friendship with Doug is something I'd pursue all over again. But maybe it's not really a *friend* I've told you about in these pages.

The tradition in which I serve confesses that, through Baptism, we are a "priesthood of all believers." We are called in Baptism to be community in which we are ministers of Jesus Christ to one another. Though he would have chuckled at the suggestion, in so many ways Doug functioned as a priest. That is, this pastor had a pastor, so to speak. He listened not simply with his ears. But with his eyes. With his heart.

Burying Doug was one of my final official acts as a pastor to that congregation. I was relocating to another call. Cynicism—when I go there—often leads me to think that congregations don't fear losing pastors. Only being without them. Being replaceable, the congregation would receive another pastor. With Doug's death we lost someone irreplaceable. Such is the value of the priesthood we shared among one another.

(10)

Self-care and Ministry

Just Love your People

I was sitting on her living room couch. Before me was a round, glass table adorned with a black, leather-bound Bible. It sat next to a small dish of red and white candy. Across the room, in the center of the east wall, was a large landscape painting. It depicted the open prairie which was typical of the landscape surrounding this community.

The room was decorated in various shades of yellow and green. Excepting the large prairie landscape painting on the east wall, the room's motif was that of flowers: floral wallpaper, a floral living room set consisting of a couch and a love seat, in addition to an over-stuffed recliner. I had been served coffee. It was good. Black. Strong. The sugar cookies I was offered complemented the coffee.

My host—I'll call her Sara, at the time in her early-80s—was tall and elegant. She had managed to maintain the brunette locks of her younger days. What strands of gray she did have served as stylish highlights. She had the vitality of a woman thirty years her junior.

Her husband's death was now five years in the past. Like so many of the farmers I came to know out there, I learned that he gave himself to his work, to his work, and then to his work. He was rarely seen without his seed cap, a flannel shirt, and his overalls. A cigarette dangling from his cigar-sized fingers completed the portrait. His cigarette habit—so he told those who knew him—was acquired just before his "walk across Europe" which began in June of 1944. Her husband, from all accounts, was a picture of rugged masculinity, a man of earth and engine grease. Together they raised two girls. It was easy to picture the women going about their lives in this floral home. The earth and engine grease, the scent of work-a-day masculinity, was difficult to conjure within these walls. The only trace of him within the home was confined to the family portrait on the credenza.

And like so many farm couples out there—in that land where trees huddle in the ravines and along the creek beds and the thunderstorms often seem like they are rolling through the attic—it was hard to believe, knowing Sara and having learned about her late husband, that these two lived in the same home together for close to fifty years. The home appeared the same as the day he died of a sudden heart attack. The Morton building out behind the house still looked on the inside as it did the day he died. So I was told.

I sat on that floral couch and listened intently. I sipped my coffee and nibbled on sugar cookies. I had learned about her life and family history. I had learned about her various commitments to church and community. And then, about fifteen minutes into my visit, it happened.

Probably due to my overemphasis on sports, I was academically uninspired during high school. Though I seldom took home books (mostly due to the scheduling of study halls), I graduated in the top fifth of my class. High school consisted of a box checking attitude regarding academic subjects. As if to say: "Check it off the list in order to graduate and play football in college." College would become a different matter entirely. Vocational direction fanned the flames of academic interest.

With seminary's arrival it seemed as if I had mainlined a dose of insatiable curiosity. I wasn't simply reading the books which were assigned. I was reading the books listed in the footnotes of the books I was assigned. I was reading the books referenced by professors during lectures and seminars. I was reading books for point. I was reading books for counterpoint. I immersed myself in New Testament monographs. And Old Testament ones. I devoured books on dogmatic, systematic, and constructive theology; books on Martin Luther's theology and John Calvin's theology. And Karl Barth. And Paul Tillich. And on and on. Some of it I absorbed. Some of it I did not. It was as if the energies of my soul had found their proper groove within the universe.

"Follow your bliss," were the words of Joseph Campbell. "Bliss" was a section of interstate upon which I was the only driver. Near the end of seminary, I was awarded a stipend for language study at the Göthe Institute in Bremen, Germany. It was the city near which, incidentally, my mother-in-law's family had resettled after World War II.

Eventually, having returned from Germany, I received a call to a congregation in a small community where the Midwest meets the Plains. I never dreamed of the psychic upheaval such a transition would provoke.

"Just love your people." Such was the advice of the bishop who connected me with my first call. So that became my goal.

And to achieve that goal—in my estimation—I had to immerse myself in the community. And to immerse myself in the community I had to visit as many homes within the congregation as I would be permitted. During these visits I learned about the community, the congregation, its families. I learned of their history and their identity. I learned about the triumphs and the traumas that had impacted and shaped them. I learned what was important. And I learned what was not important. With the sharing of life stories came relationships. Each visit involved long conversation. And prayer. And the Lord's Supper. By the time I had departed my first call four years later I could tell you the names of most of the congregation's family members two and three generations back. The congregation consisted of approximately 450 members.

And it was because of this plan that I found myself in Sara's floral living room, on her couch, drinking coffee and eating sugar cookies. And it was there, on that couch by that glass table, as Sara was detailing her life story, that I was slowly captured by a feeling of unease. It wasn't fear that I felt. It was more like a sense that I had been gradually losing control. Over what I wasn't sure.

My concentration had become diffuse. I was no longer able to focus with undivided attention on Sara's voice. It wasn't panic that I felt. It was more like a general dissolution of concentration and energy. My pulse had quickened. Yet I felt lethargic. Some beads of sweat slid past my temples. Slowly I sat back into that floral couch.

Feeling like I was in uncharted waters, I thought to myself: "Is this what a heart attack feels like?" I immediately answered myself: "I couldn't possibly be having a heart attack. I'm 27 and five years out of college football. And my last physical resulted in a clean bill of health. My chest isn't tight. And there are no pains in my arms, shoulders, and chest."

"Breathe in, breathe out," I said to myself. "Just breathe. This I can control." "Just think about how much you love flowers. Grandma Anthony filled her quilts with flowers. Focus on their beauty. And smile. Smile and your body will follow. This I can control."

And Sara kept sharing her story. And I kept mustering as much concentration as I could. I tried to make my countenance correspond to the ebb and flow of her tone and gestures.

I lost track of time. Precisely, if *chronos* is sequential, clock time, and *kairos* is divinely appointed time, time lost in the unity of subject and object, then the time I gradually began to experience in Sara's home fit into neither of these categories. Sequential time disappeared. Yet it felt isolating, infernal. It had become a time dedicated to self-preservation. I managed to pull myself together for prayer and Communion. The visit wrapped-up.

"You look tired," she said.

I gave her a hug and walked to the car. I took a few moments to gather myself behind the steering wheel. I drove the ten or so blocks back to the parsonage. Eventually my pulse slowed to a normal rate. What followed was a feeling of exhaustion that permeated every layer of my being.

Having arrived back home from errands, my wife looked at me and asked if I was alright. "You look beyond tired." I was experiencing a level of tired I had never experienced before. That night I slept on the couch. It was where I landed when I arrived home from Sara's house.

"Just love your people." So, the bishop had directed me upon receiving my call to serve the congregation. Now it was up to me to figure out how keep from adding the words "to death" to that sentence.

Oddly, though, this episode became a gift, the gift of a journey, one of self-discovery, of healing and wholeness. And how it all related to ordained ministry.

I am no clinical expert on anxiety and depression. But I can speak as a layman from experience. Thus, with experience in tow (along with a bit of reading), there are few things I can say about anxiety and depression.

First, regarding anxiety and depression, if the former feels like the nervous system at high tide, the latter is the same nervous system at low tide. If the former feels like a relentless wave of unchanneled energy, then the latter is a swale of that same energy's absence. The maelstrom and the doldrums form a one-two punch which leaves one hobbling.

Second, though there is a good chance one has gradually been working up to this point, it can seem as if it has dropped in like an in-law with no boundaries. It doesn't care what you are doing. It becomes all-consuming. And then it subsides. Sort of. That is, in the sense that it leaves a wake which must be navigated.

Finally, anxiety and depression appear to be correlated with—among other causes—major life changes, big events, and stressful situations. With profound change comes a challenge to one's sense of competence and control. I was a prime candidate for this one-two punch.

"You've endured profound change." Pausing for a few beats and then speaking, that was my father's response.

For a couple weeks I attempted to work from the midst of this malaise, to rouse myself day after a day for a full slate of home visits. Following the visits I would organize my office, conduct exegesis for sermons, and prepare for and facilitate Bible studies. I would then return home and attempt the office of husband.

Day after day I strained to put one foot in front of the other, to follow a thought with another thought. Day after day I attempted to manufacture even a breeze for my own sails through coffee and cold showers and positive thinking and brute determination. And day after day I felt as if I were an engine that couldn't leave first gear.

The thoughts that detained me during those weeks ran the spectrum from "It's all in my head" to "I'm slowly dying." And I was too embarrassed to confide in my wife either end of this spectrum. Telling your wife in a young marriage that you feel you are either descending into crazy or dying is no easy matter. She was still getting accustomed to the reality that I forget to close the bathroom door.

Hence the phone call to my father. He was a mental health professional. We were close. I could confide in him. He could give me insight.

"Dad," I said in the phone call, "I have a problem. And I need your help."

"What is it?"

I described to Dad what I had been experiencing. I narrated what had occurred at Sara's home. I described the sense of exhaustion and the loss of concentration. He listened intently. Dad always listened loudly.

I finished. There was a pause. And then Dad spoke.

"You've endured profound change."

"What do you mean, Dad?"

"Well, you're an intense person. And you've pressed hard in seminary. You've been feeding your passion these past several years. And you've studied overseas. And you've moved from the Twin Cities to California to the Twin Cities to Nebraska to Germany and back to Nebraska. And now out to your first call. All within a couple of years. And you've never lived in a small town before this. You're in a new context with a new set of timelines and a new horizon."

Dad continued, "You've experienced a lot of transition and change in a short amount of time. You've been operating at a high level." He paused, "And now you've had to switch gears. Things are moving at a slower pace for a mind that works quickly and life that has been in overdrive. I'm wondering whether there was something about that visit, its mood, its pacing, that offered perspective about what ministry is all about and subsequently triggered your anxiety. You've gone from theological lectures and writing papers to committee meetings and home visitations. That's a hell of a change. It may feel like you've lost some of the control over life you once thought you possessed." He added, "And you've probably been questioning your competence for ministry."

He continued, "As well, you're an athlete. You've never had to think about it all these years. When change and the possibility of anxiety came along you were playing football. You were running and lifting and practicing and playing in games. Athletics was taking your mind off the day's worries. You were burning energy and releasing endorphins. You were keeping your mind clear. In seminary, as I understand, you continued to run and lift weights. Have you been exercising at all recently?"

Come to think of it, the answer was no. "No" audibly slipped from my lips.

Dad added, "Start with long walks. Walk with your wife. Walk at night, just before bedtime. It'll burn some of the energy and clear the mind. A big night sky can put life in perspective. Walking can also heal a relationship that has been tested by all those moves and transitions. At some point start lifting weights again. Your body and your mind are one fabric. Don't forget that."

"And remember," Dad said, "you are whole and you are prepared for this. You are where you need to be. And you are more than competent. Remember though: you must tend to your own needs before you can tend to the needs of others."

He added, his words striking with a gentle sharpness, "And don't self-medicate."

I paused a long pause. I felt exposed. "Ok, Dad."

Dad's directive was clear: the season had arrived for the cultivation of self-awareness and the healing which can grow from it. Not self-medicating. We can't heal that which we self-medicate.

I had been flirting, like I always had, with the self-medicating option. It had been a time-tested form of self-soothing which had always *almost* worked. Dad spoke to one who was beginning to venture down this path again. Not everyone can make a phone call to a father who happens to be a mental health professional.

I have drunk alcohol to round off the sharp edges of anxiety. I have drunk alcohol to medicate depression. I have drunk alcohol to quell feelings of insecurity and social awkwardness. I have drunk alcohol to fit in. I have drunk alcohol out of boredom. I have drunk alcohol to numb grief. I have drunk alcohol to induce a feeling of connection to . . . *exactly what I could not tell you.*

I have come to think of addiction in general as an attempt to seek a wholeness which already exists. We are convinced by experience, by pain, by loss of control, that something fundamental is missing. We begin our lives whole and complete. Life's traumas and adversities and alienations can hard-wire within us a counter claim. Is it any surprise that—already on the first page of the Bible—humanity is declared to be created in the image of God? that, from the get-go, we are divinely loved into the image of the Divine Love? We are whole from the beginning. Now we just need to be convinced of the matter.

Perhaps what the church has historically called The Fall revolves, at least in part, around a perpetual attempt—collectively and individually—to convince ourselves in thought, word, and deed, that the love of God—and the wholeness which issues from it—is a reward and not our origin. We are created in the image of that God. *Tōv meōd.* Exceedingly good. It is a radical message. Already on the first page of the Bible.

Never once has an evening of drinking reached its intended goal. The situation which existed prior to drinking remains when the drinking is concluded. Only now with a hangover and a feeling of generalized anxiety which intensifies the concerns I originally aimed to chemically diminish. What is more, as I have learned, to medicate with alcohol is tantamount to attempting to consume enough of something that *almost* works. One never quite gets enough of that which doesn't quite do the job. One becomes trapped in a cognitive dissonance of sorts: continuing to embrace alcohol's medicinal promise while wandering amid the ruins it has left in its path.

There was a sign on a bus stop bench in St. Paul, Minnesota I read once years ago in my late teens which—claiming to quote Abraham Lincoln—declared that "Alcohol has many defenders and no defense." That message has always remained with me. At eighteen I laughed off such words. As an ordained clergyperson for 25+ years I no longer laugh at such a claim.

Alcohol quelled social anxiety during my early-20s. Alcohol greased the rails of all of life's transitions during my middle and late-20s. Alcohol took the edge off through deadlines and uncertainties of the Ph.D. process in my early-30s. The year I was pastoring, finishing my dissertation (started on June 1 and completed on December 23 of that year), and teaching three courses in religion at a college down the road was filled with self-medicating with alcohol.

At the risk of sounding preachy, it needs to be addressed . . .

It may well be a truism that the higher up the academic ladder one climbs, the less stigmatized heavy drinking becomes. Seminaries and divinity schools are not immune from this reality simply because of their subject matter. A colleague once confided in me that it wasn't the level of reading he wasn't prepared for in his Ph.D. program, but the level of drinking which was accepted among his academic peers and professors at social gatherings. "I couldn't keep up," he asserted with exasperation, "with the drinking!"

But why *wouldn't* seminaries and divinity schools be Petri dishes for heavy drinking? If a Petri dish contains a culture which is intended to facilitate the flourishing of the specimen it contains, then such institutions fit the bill. That is, if heavy drinking is associated with such matters as stress, anxiety and depression, perfectionism, transition, insecurity, and struggles with identity, then such environments become optimum places for nurturing such behavior.

They are transformational contexts in which new vocations emerge from old ones. Such places witness the evolution of identities and the upheaval which is involved in such a process. They are contexts of self-doubt: is this call to seminary/divinity school really a calling from God? Am I really suited for this vocation? Is all this theology stuff really for me? Do I measure-up to my professors' expectations? Do I really want to take a cut in compensation in relation to my previous vocation? Do I really *love the Lord* this much? As environments of transition and transformation, competition, and insecurity, seminaries and divinity schools can be rife with psychic pain. As such, the attempt to medicate such pain is often translated into the cultivation of drinking habits which can be difficult to reverse once their tracks have been laid-down.

Students working in such a context will do many things to fit in with their peers. And professors can often be esteemed to the point of adulation, admired to the point of emulation. Adulation and emulation often become the avenue by which we seek to be embraced by those who teach us and evaluate our work. They write our recommendations.

On the matter of adulation and emulation: a popular seminary professor of mine—confident, intelligent, urbane—was widely known for his pipe smoking. Indeed, to converse with him in his office was a smorgasbord for the senses: eyes filled with shelves of theological tomes, ears flooded with theological pearls, hands taking notes feverishly, coffee sipped during pauses, and . . . the lingering aroma of Virginia #7. That was the tobacco he smoked. I know because I asked. And, hence, that was the tobacco we smoked in our pipes on the roof of student housing at night. With a tumbler of single malt Scotch or Kentucky bourbon. And let us not forget the intelligent-sounding dialogue conducted theological neophytes. All of it out of adulation and emulation. I was playing the part, so-to-speak.

To the point: if seminaries and divinity schools are the crucible for theological/ministry formation, then it would be wise to also consider them as contexts for modeling self-awareness and self-care, especially as it relates to understanding and addressing the transformation, the psychic upheaval, which occurs in such contexts.

And then consider: the product of such environments will be called to minister to communities soaked in multiple levels of psychic pain produced by family systems mired in addiction, anxiety and depression, guilt and shame, profound tragedies, and physical and emotional abuse. A pastor can either be an accomplice to a congregation's various expressions of pain, or a seer, and thus a possible healing presence, regarding such pain.

Ultimately, one of the most powerful instruments in a pastor's repertoire is a growing awareness of one's own inner states. It is an awareness which, in turn, permits one to recognize and minister to those states in others. The pastor's path to ministering to the wounds of others runs first through seeing, naming, standing within, and mercifully tending to their own. I can't see and feel my way into, I can't tend to, the psychic pain in others I have self-medicated. I can't extend love's vigilance and grace's healing to others if I have not first extended it inward.

God's gifts are delivered in the most unexpected of wrapping. I will always give thanks for the "Sara Visit" and what it initiated. It became the catalyst for addressing psychic pain. From the "Sara Visit" came an invitation to compassionately cultivate an inward gaze which corresponds to the one by which I am seen by God. It has been my experience that this inward gaze births a corresponding gaze outward, one issuing in a more empathetic understanding of those I serve.

In our wounds—their naming and healing—stirs the promise of developing our humanizing capacities. A pastor's most powerful gift may well be resurrected from within a personal tomb which can often appear too painful and dark to enter. We can avoid that tomb and medicate. Or Christ's love and mercy can spill into it. The "light shines in the darkness" (John 1: 5). Even this darkness.

"Minister from your wounds." Those were the words of a beloved mentor. The words were addressed to me as a young pastor. Though uninvited, such wounds bear the promise of becoming—through an inward gaze animated by Christ's mercy and the sacrament of healing time—sober tutors for the vocation of ministry. It is a Spirit-animated gaze which becomes the touchstone for seeing and serving the people to whom we are called to minister. They, too, are created in image of the Divine Love, its wholeness.

"Minister," my mentor lovingly advised, "from your wounds." From them grows the embrace of our own humanity. And the recognition of that humanity in others.

(11)

Church and Politics

Church in the Time of Trump

The envelope had arrived in the mail. My secretary had placed it in my church mailbox. It was now sitting on my desk. The name and return address on the envelope indicated something was amiss. This was a family that communicated matters in person. With my pocket knife I cut it open along the top. Inside the envelope was a single piece of folded paper. I unfolded it. I placed it on my desk. Below its dateline this is what had been typed:

> Please discontinue the automatic $20 weekly contribution from our checking account to the church. We will be closing the account on which this is drawn.
>
> We refuse to support groups who are sanctuary organizations in defiance of the laws of our land and the U.S. Constitution out of hatred for President Trump.
>
> I recently read somewhere: 'If a church changes their values to match current culture, then they are *no longer following the Bible* [italics his], but following the lost.' (Amen)
>
> Thank you,
>
> Joe Q. Smith

I folded the letter back up. I placed it back in the envelope. A litany of thoughts lit up my mind.

The first thought, I'm sorry to say, was immature. It went something like this: "Take your measly $20 and shove it somewhere dark." I moved quickly past this sentiment. Such a thought is a waste of time and energy. As well, such an attitude is not expressive of the person I try to be each day.

I was reminded of the wealthy old parishioner who told me that he was indefinitely withholding his tithe because the congregation had voted to remodel the church entrance to facilitate access for those with physical disabilities. Maintaining the integrity of the original church building was more important for him than its accessibility. I'm sure that pastors distribute the Lord's Supper to parishioners like this one all the time.

My second thought was to call the man, to gain some perspective, perhaps gently challenge him to see matters differently. It was a fleeting thought. His letter left no room for conversation. A caricature of this man was conjured in my mind—like one of those distorted drawings one might sit for at a state fair—of a disproportionately small head, smaller ears, and a gaping mouth that was twice the size of his face. All of it sitting atop little body attired in red, white, and blue. All of it adorned with a yellow ribbon.

The third thought that crossed my mind—the one which ultimately informed my response—was this: "His real religion has been revealed. Move on. Give thanks for the revelation. And give thanks that the vine has been cleansed."

Notice, I used the word *religion*. Let me substitute the word *narrative*. As in, "The *narrative* by which he has identified himself had been revealed." For too long, it seems, he was—like many—able to conceal the matter. In this case, I was later told, it took a post-synod assembly protest in the upper-Midwest near an Immigration and Customs Enforcement (ICE) facility to draw his self-identifying *narrative* out of concealment.

I am convinced—among other dynamics I have observed as a pastor during this era—that the "Time of Trump" is something of a fuller unmasking of competing narratives (along with their corresponding identities) which our collective civility façade once (somewhat) concealed. But had we not detected cracks in the façade during the run-up to the "Time of Trump"? The tribal, polarized incivility of public discourse—certainly intensified by social media and the ease and anonymity of communication it facilitates, in addition to the echo chambers it creates—in which we are immersed didn't begin with him. It is my sense that the "Time of Trump" is a symptom of the dark vitalities which have long stirred and festered deep in our collective psyche. Borrowing the metaphor from this book's introduction: high heels and make-up will no longer hide any of it. Is it even possible to elaborate *a* narrative which unites Americans? Or are we sentenced as a nation to a long, chronic, internecine war of competing narratives which continues to drive us farther into an abyss of hostility and disintegration?

But the question on the table, at least for the sake of the theme around which this chapter is organized, is this: as many of us have come to observe that there are apparently such things as *red* and *blue* Christians, is it possible to articulate a narrative—grounded in the ministry of Jesus Christ—which bears the promise of uniting those same Christians? Is it even possible to articulate *a* Christianity which is not simply a façade for other, more fundamental identity-determining commitments?

We have come through an epoch—philosophers have indicated—that has been coined "postmodernity." One of the signature attributes of postmodernity is its suspicion of, its incredulity toward, metanarratives, or overarching stories which provide a shared sense of identity and meaning.[1]

Concretely (and certainly oversimplified), and framed within the American context, though millions of Americans may celebrate the "land of the free," millions more shake their heads and declare, "Not our story." As in: "Our people were brought to this continent as those sold into slavery and lived for generations as chattel laborers, only to then endure—having been allegedly freed by a war—an atmosphere of racial animus and Jim Crow laws." And let us note: such an atmosphere was not confined to the South. Such phenomena as "redlining" and "sundown towns" occurred across the United States deep into the 20th century. Again, though many will celebrate a narrative of freedom, many others will identify themselves with the long, dehumanizing narrative of racism and discrimination. But what has also become clear, such dehumanization also hides within a veneer of virtue and good intentions.

Dehumanization is also conducted with a *kiss*. Paternalism's *kiss*.[2] It is the subtle dehumanization—masked by virtue and good intentions—that

---

1. See Lyotard, *The Postmodern Condition*

2. An exhibit on slavery several years ago at the *National WWI Museum and Memorial* in Kansas City revealed a shocking, sobering slogan articulated by Democrat party leaders to the Black population in the South following the Civil War. Though I don't remember the slogan exactly, here is its paraphrased form: "Vote Democrat or end up in a wooden coat." The words are troubling to ponder. But such a logic, in subtler form, has not disappeared from our national discourse. On a radio show hosted by *Charlamagne tha God* I shuddered to hear then presidential candidate Biden declare with regard to options for president in 2020, "Well, I tell you what, if you have a problem figuring out whether you're for me or Trump, then you ain't Black." He followed this declaration up

asserts, "We know more about your needs than you do, we know what is best for you." As if to say: when the dehumanizing force of *overt racism* is no longer socially accepted or legal, then wield the subtle, infantilizing power of *covert racism*. Both dehumanize. The latter is concealed under the veil of virtue and good intentions. Should we not always be asking: in addition to continually striving for an atmosphere of equality/equal rights, how do we serve one another in such a manner that the humanity of the other is empowered? How we do learn to see one another through the lens of empowerment, and not merely as objects/classes to be exploited for the sake of power?

What is more: though many identify with the narrative of "picking one's self up by the bootstraps," others remind us that "it takes a village." Though many identify with the narrative of "hard work" which "creates opportunities," others remind us of denied opportunities and glass ceilings. Though many speak of a deep identity "in the land," others among us remind us of a "land" which has been reduced to reservations. A suspicion of metanarratives is engendered and framed by the recognition of communities, their narratives, which have historically been reduced to a marginalized status, rendered invisible by another, *official* narrative.

But it is here that I offer an alternative perspective on metanarratives, one certainly filtered through my pastor-lens. That is, perhaps it is not metanarratives, *per se*, we must be suspicious of, but metanarratives wielded as instruments of power, division, and dehumanization. These are the metanarratives fueled by retribution and fed by victims sacrificed at the altar of such things as race and ethnicity, ideology, economy, and gender. A metanarrative can be humanizing, uniting, and healing. A metanarrative can serve to dehumanize, divide, and destroy.

Could one—and here my idealism gushes forth—make the case that identity as Americans is derived from perpetually discovering together,

---

with, "take a look at my record, man!" The words were cringeworthy. And his record of past comments surrounding race didn't help. But more than this: it appears—and convince me to the contrary—that both the post-Civil War slogan and Biden's comments were informed by the same logic of racism with the former expressing its overt form and the latter its subtler, covert form. It was a sober reminder for me that racism is able to conceal itself in the well-intentioned guise of paternalism. Such is the ability of virtue to conceal matters from self-awareness. What is more: racism is not tied to political parties—as no party has a corner on the racism market, but hearts and minds. What I long to hear more clearly from any party is this: equality, empowerment, and opportunity as equals should be denied no one because of race, ethnicity/nationality, sexual orientation, gender, creed, et. al.

living into, the capacious nature of such realities as equality, equal rights, and "life, liberty, and the pursuit of happiness"? What if we were continually called to discover together the collective empowerment our founders miraculously (given their context) envisioned through the mode of self-government coined a federal constitutional representative democracy? In short: what if America's greatness was animated not by a longing for returning to a Fata Morgana-like golden era, but its desire to work toward a perpetual state of humanization and empowerment amid its diversity? Maybe I'm just a hopeless idealist.

In a country of diversity and abundance, it appears that we have often approached such matters as equality and opportunity from a zero-sum perspective. A world viewed through a zero-sum lens sees diversity either as a threat, or as reality to be exploited for the sake of power (normally by pitting identified classes against each other). A world viewed through a zero-sum lens always sees abundance refracted through the logic of scarcity. Resentment—the nursing and exploiting of resentments—is the drug which fuels the zero-sum enterprise.

I never saw or spoke to either the man or his family after I received his letter. I have thought of them often. I harbor no malice toward them. Such a manner of thinking only poisons the one who harbors it. As well, the God who sustains me also sustains his family. God's blessings are not handed-out according to zero-sum logic.

And though his letter—as evidenced by its opening decision, its terseness; its righteous, uncompromising, patriotic parlance—expressed no willingness to cede space for discussion, I have thought often of answering. No doubt such a message would fall on deaf ears, so to speak. Regardless, I have formulated an answer. The answer is not intended for him. It is too long. It's intended for me. It's an opportunity express my own understanding of *church* in such tribalized, polarized, resentful times. Here it goes . . .

> Dear Joe,
>
> I was saddened by the message I received from you recently. I was saddened for a couple of reasons.
>
> The first is this: I always enjoyed worshiping with you. I enjoyed our conversations following worship, your questions, your insights.
>
> The second is this: it has always been a policy of mine as a pastor to have an "open door." In this case, I have always indicated my willingness to listen to concerns and frustrations. Through

conversation new vistas emerge. That opportunity is behind us now. I mourn that fact.

It has come to my attention that you were angered by clergy-voiced opposition directed at I.C.E. officials following a recent synodical convention. It has come to my attention that you were angered by the hostility directed at Republicans/conservatives—certainly Trump and Trump supporters—by many clergy/lay people of our denomination. I do have deep concerns that our church body has begun to mirror the toxic rhetoric and divisiveness many of its members claim to detest. And I would have welcomed a conversation about this.

But I also want to take this opportunity to express a few points per your letter.

First, as elaborated by both the Old and New Testaments, it is a fundamental expression of Christian discipleship to protect, to provide hospitality for, the most vulnerable among us no matter who they are. Through the Holy Spirit we have been called in Jesus Christ who is our identity to prioritize the vulnerable; to give a voice to those whose voices have been suppressed. All other identities are penultimate to this Christ-identity.

I completely agree: let us not "follow the lost" (your term) in elevating to ultimate value penultimate realities. If need be, may this vigilance for the vulnerable always find the Christian church at odds with "current culture" (your term).

We could have shared our frustrations over the reality that it has often appeared that the Christian church in America has permitted its identity in Jesus Christ to become an optional identity and not an identifying one. As well, we could have shared together a conversation regarding the motivation and nature of our country's laws, the enforcement of those laws, how to think about those laws from the perspective of the Lordship of Jesus Christ.

Second, I am disappointed that your religious indignation is only ignited when the "laws of our land and the U.S. Constitution" are perceived to be disrespected. Is it ok when Christians are more deeply versed in political party platforms than in our own Bible and creeds? Is it ok when Christian beliefs/commitments are edited to fit our political platforms?

Having attempted to make of nation and God two, equally-weighted commitments, maybe you have learned that one can't serve two masters simultaneously. A prayerful conversation may have provided an occasion to clarify the nature, in addition to their ordering, of these commitments.

Finally, let us not become the evil we abhor. That is, in this politically tribal time, with its suffocating atmosphere of resentment and hatred-filled, divisive rhetoric; with its exchange of the One, True God for the vengeance-fueled gods of nationalism, political and intersectional tribalism, and wealth, and power—et. al.!—it is easy to become the very darkness we perceive in others. When this happens the followers of Christ lose their Gospel-funded initiative and identity. Instead, we become reactionaries on the world's terms and conditions. Instead of being a ground, we become conductors of the world's retributive currents. And so the Christian church loses its distinction from society at large. We are not called to mirror the world. We are called to subvert it—together—through Christ's mercy.

Ultimately, though I have no leverage by which to make this request, I ask only one thing from you: repent daily that you may rise with Christ as his servant. And be a blessing of God's love and mercy to your new Christ fellowship. As a temple of Christ's love, continue to be an instrument of God's blessings to our community. Though we are no longer united by worship and fellowship, let us remain united as living rewards to those around us in the community, friend and foe alike.

This letter was longer than I originally planned. Such is the occupational temptation of a pastor.

Peace + Joy + Love,

Pastor Anthony

+ + + + + + +

There was a point at which I lamented the "Time of Trump." But I also give thanks for the clarity which has emerged during this season. Matters once hidden, especially regarding core commitments and their corresponding identities, have been revealed. And it has revealed those—both *blue* and *red*—for whom *Christian* was something more like a veneer concealing retribution-fueled ideologies. But there is something even more disturbing which I have observed during the "Time of Trump."

Many who have claimed to be disgusted by Trump have all too effortlessly expressed the rhetoric and behavior they claim to abhor. Many have all too effortlessly become the monster they have claimed to despise. All too effortlessly. It's as if another's attributes have served as nothing more than a lure which has caused similar ones to rise from our own depths.

Indeed, the "Time of Trump" has informed the development of my own definition of *magical thinking*. It is the belief that more of the same will eliminate the *sameness* that delivered us to this point. That is, *magical thinking* is evil's *coup de grâce*, its complete colonizing of people by animating them with the retributive logic by which they have been provoked and dehumanized. As if to say, "not only have I provoked, even dehumanized you, I've also captured your mind and heart with my logic. I've now wired you to do unto others what I have done to unto you."

Such *magical thinking* convinces us that just one more convincing display of retribution will magically deliver us to the portal of peace. Confusing a difference in degree for a difference in kind, we only serve to push the reset button on retribution, thus further securing evil's dominion. And retribution's lordship, though remaining on the devil's continuum of authority, is veiled in the *virtuous* and the *holy*. Its disciples even call upon Jesus to bless the retributive spirit which crucified him.

+ + + + + + +

The "Time of Trump" seems to have awakened that least desirable part of us we thought we had suppressed. It was that part of us which we thought we could keep concealed from others under the façade of *civilized society*. Or perhaps under a veneer of empathy. Yet the "Time of Trump" bears the warning that we cannot deny the existence of the dragon loitering beneath the surface of our identities. For to do so comes with a price. Namely, self-devourment. As individuals. As a people. We cast onto others the dark vitalities which stir at our core.

The "Time of Trump" poses a question to those who identify themselves with the church of Jesus Christ: has a confession of the crucified and risen Christ been carved-up to fit a prior, more fundamental identity (a political party, a race, an ethnicity, an ideology, et. al.)? Shall we give thanks for the opportunity of discernment such a season offers? Christ's healing only begins where our alienation from Jesus Christ has been named and owned.

It is in the painful, Holy Spirit-animated process of coming to self-awareness and cultivating self-criticism that the beauty of Christ's ministry of reconciliation flowers most fully. Is there a prelude to Christ's hallelujah which circumvents such a process? Placed within the context of our fundamental act of worship: liturgy—no matter how well it is planned, vested, and orchestrated—is neither theater nor an appeal for the divine sanctioning of our tribal and retributive tendencies, but the medium by which the life-giving Word of God is proclaimed and encountered unto a "new creation" beyond the destructive distinctions and divisions of this world (Gal. 6:15).

We confess that we are saved by *grace alone*. Such grace—Jesus Christ—is both the source of our self-awareness and the promise of the humanity God intends for us. It is a humanity created in the image of that same God.

(12)

The Church and Biblical Interpretation

The Promise of Humor

"And I tell you, you are Peter, and on this rock I will build my church, and the gates of Hades will not prevail against it." (Matt 16:18)

The debate over this verse gradually intensified. The promise of a lunch together at a local Chinese buffet on the south end of town prevented disagreement from morphing into open rancor. It was during that text study—one of those weekly gatherings in which area colleagues check-in, pray together, and share insights regarding the upcoming Sunday's prescribed preaching texts—that two, veteran pastors got into it over the meaning, and thus the application, of this passage. In so many ways one's interpretation of this passage served as something of a litmus test among colleagues. Are they authentically Lutheran? Are they Lutheran in name only?

The one old pastor to my right indicated that Peter's name—*Petros* in Koine Greek—means *rock*. It is only logical, he continued, that Jesus intended this designation to mean that Peter (*Petros*) is the *rock* upon which the One, Holy, Catholic, and Apostolic Church was founded. *This*, he asserted, is the literal meaning of this passage. What is more, he asserted, such a meaning reinforces the idea that a church body—for it to be considered authentically Christian—should be able to trace its lineage of bishops back to *this* bishop, or Peter, *Petros*, the *rock*, the foundation of the church's authority. This—he contended—is what is intended by the term *Apostolic* (as in: the One, Holy, Catholic, and Apostolic Church).

The second old pastor, sitting directly across the table from me, having quietly, yet restively, listened to the aforementioned interpretation and application of the passage, sat up and cleared his throat. "We all see that. Yes, but let me point out to you that the term *rock* was employed a second time, just a sentence clause later." Pointing out that the second employment of the term *rock* was spelled differently and placed in the lower-case in the original language (*petra*), he developed a line of argument that ran as such: "What the writer of the Gospel of Matthew is telling us is that the church is not built upon Peter (*Petros*), but instead the *rock* (*petra*) of our confession of Jesus Christ as Lord." "Hence," he continued, "from this is grounded the truth that the church is founded on the confession of the Word of God, and thus the proper understanding and administration of Word and Sacrament which is conducted from and for that confession."

Again, at risk of expressing the matter simplistically, but certainly filtered through the conversations of the time, what this pastor essentially elaborated was a classic, Protestant rebuttal to the assertion that Peter is the first installment in an unbroken succession—of teaching and preaching, the authority to do so—upon which the *true* church is founded. With this latter interpretation the dynamics of authority remain, though shifted—we might say—from a lineage-based emphasis to a theological one.

At the time such exchanges over Peter and rocks became heated for ecumenical reasons. The church body to which I belong—again, risking a simplistic treatment of the matter—had agreed (as a condition of being considered in full communion with another church body) to accepting the Historic Episcopate[1] as an expression of visible unity. Though a churchwide decision had been made, conversation and controversy remained within the ranks of clergy: was the Historic Episcopate a necessity or something more of an indulgence presented as one? The question was asked among many of my colleagues: what is *enough* for Christian *unity*? Is it the ability to trace a church body's leadership—*bishops*, the same authorities many once called *presidents*—lineage back to Peter (*Petros*)? Or is it a proper administration of Word and Sacrament conducted from and for the confession (*petra*) of

---

1. Profoundly simplified: that our church body's bishops—once called *presidents* in some of its feeder bodies—be recognized in an unbroken line of historical succession traced back to the Apostles in the New Testament.

the Word of God? Simply, where is the *visible unity* of the Christian church located? As many of my colleagues suspected, lurking behind the matter of visible unity was the question of *authority*. Where it is located and, subsequently, how is the church organized around it? More on that in a bit.

What did you say? A professor of theology in my tradition once remarked regarding the implications of the aforementioned controversy—having considered that the church body with which my own was considering full communion was declining in membership—that committing to full communion with them was tantamount to "ecclesiastical necrophilia." Irreverent. Harsh. Perhaps containing a kernel of truth. I understand his comment even made the pages of well-known periodical.

Indeed, the church body to which I belong, the Evangelical Lutheran Church in America (ELCA)—formed by the merger of three church bodies on January 1, 1988—has never experienced a sustained period of increased membership ("baptized membership"). In 1988 it consisted of over 5,250,000 baptized members. By 2017 baptized membership was just north of 3,450,000. As of 2021—the most recent figures I could find—it consisted of just over 3,000,000 baptized members. A study conducted by the ELCA's Office of Research and Evaluation has projected that by 2050 the ELCA will consist of fewer than 67,000 members. The study has projected that by 2041 this church body will average 16,000 in worship across all its synods in the United States.[2] The projections are sobering. But not shocking.

But let us be careful, lest we begin worshiping at the altar of quantitative data. Such figures don't capture the nature of God's agency and commitment to the church. Let us remember: not only is ours a Lord whose lordship is revealed in suffering-unto-death, but—by the time we arrive at the foot of the cross in the Gospels—it seems obvious that *quantity* of members plays second-fiddle to the demonstration of God the Son's commitment to revealing the depth of God's love for God's people. I will say more on the *membership* issue in a bit.

Both of those old pastors at the text study were correct. Peter (*Petros*) is the *rock* upon which the Christian church is founded. As well, his confession (*petra*) of the Lord corresponds to his *rock*-like status. Both *Petros* and *petra* are equally expressions of the nature of the church's authority. But that is indeed what makes this whole debate so—dare I say—funny. And such is

---

2. See Zscheile, "Will the ELCA be Gone in 30 Years?" In this article Zscheile references the aforementioned study.

the reason why—as I will develop—both gentlemen were both correct yet wildly off the mark.

Though I'm getting ahead of myself, it must be asked: as those who confess the God revealed in Jesus Christ to be the unilateral author and agent of creation, redemption, and sanctification, wouldn't it be natural to suspect that even a modicum of humor (and a corresponding sense of humility) should inform the church's self-awareness? How many theological courses and tomes have communicated the matter that proper theology issues in a proper sense of humor and humility?

It may be the case that the absence of a such a disposition is a key symptom of the sickness which festers throughout many expressions of church. That sickness, derived from a chronic quest to seek justification apart from Jesus Christ, expresses itself by means of many symptoms. They are (but not limited to): the inclination to seek justification by right institutional expression alone, or by right biblical interpretation alone, or by right theology/doctrine alone, or by right liturgy alone, or by right social justice stance alone, or by right political party affiliation alone. It is a sickness which, ultimately, consumes its sufferers by some species of right hierarchy alone. Once the organizing principle of the hierarchy is determined the matter of determining royalty and courtiers takes care of itself.

Let us not forget: Sarah did laugh (Gen 18:13ff.). No doubt because she was thinking of the condition of her reproductive organs at age 90. Her son is the child of this laughter. Laughter occurs in the discrepancy between awareness of reality and God's promise. If laughter doesn't occur, perhaps one of the two has not been fully grasped.

If Peter is the *rock* upon which Jesus founds his church, then such a designation is not a *prescription* for the church to anchor its authority on either a purity of lineage (Historic Episcopate) or a purity of theology (right teaching and administering of Word and Sacrament). It is a *description* of the people *called out* (*ecclesia*) to conduct his ministry. Don't get me wrong: such a matter as lineage is important for a church which understands itself to be One, Holy, Catholic, and *Apostolic*. And it is necessary that servants of Word and Sacrament be educated thoroughly within their respective theological traditions. But such matters as lineage and theology are expressions of the crucified and risen Lord who has called us. And both are shot through to the core with sin.

Thus, if Peter is to be considered *Petros*, and what he confesses is *petra*, it is nothing more than Jesus' employment of humor—a grace jest in our direction—in the service of describing a core, collective personality trait embodied by Peter's church. It is a fundamental characteristic of the people upon whom Jesus Christ has no choice but to build his church.

Ultimately, I contend, Peter and his church are how Jesus Christ will reveal the radical nature of his commitment and mercy. The church's authority is not grounded on a competence Jesus Christ discerns within it, but the competence he imparts to it through the Holy Spirit. But it is also a short, easy step from worshiping Jesus Christ and serving the world through Jesus Christ . . . to masking hubris with that same Jesus Christ. How I can say such a thing? More on that in a moment.

The other Lutherans in that small town practiced closed communion. *Closed* was certainly a termed associated with communion practice. But its impact was wider than that. Its tentacles reached deeply into families, working down through the generations. Split families split communities.

Closed meant that if you grew up in the *other* Lutheran church yet married into our Lutheran church, then you had disqualified yourself from communing at the church in which you were baptized and confirmed. Even though the entire rest of your family worshiped at the *other* Lutheran church, you were banned from communing with them at the church of your spiritual weaning. One who married into our Lutheran congregation could enjoy intimacy with their spouse, but not the Sacrament of Holy Communion offered by Jesus Christ at their original—more doctrinally *pure*—congregation.

It was an internalized truism of the *other* Lutherans that a family had to give up *true* Communion for a Sunday if they wanted to commune with a family member who happened to marry a member of our congregation. It was often the case that those from the *other* Lutheran congregation would worship with us while rejecting the offer to commune at our table. Nothing more Christ-like than rejecting fellow Christians at the core of their worship! The tribalistic identity grounded in doctrinally-derived purity reinforced by the practice of closed Communion superseded the priority of our baptismal, Christ-identity.

I'll never forget the elderly woman who—having married into the Lutheran congregation I was serving—directed her giving to her old congregation, the *other* Lutheran church. Her husband did not give of his finances, time, or talent to his congregation. Both were deeply concerned that sermons remain under ten minutes.

One of my good friends during that call, an elder at the *other* Lutheran congregation, once indicated over a game of pool and cocktails in his basement, that there were "too goddamned many Pharisees" in his church. "And we wonder why our church is shrinking," he added. "Just a bunch of old farts like me. And soon we'll be gone. With nothing but a nice building to show for it."

We now return to that text study table, just before our lunch. "Blessed are you, Simon son of Jonah!"—Jesus Christ declares to Peter upon his confession that Jesus is "the Christ, the Son of the living God"—"For flesh and blood has not revealed this to you, but my Father in heaven! And I tell you, you are Peter [*Petros*], and on this rock [*petra*] I will build my church. And the gates of Hades will not prevail against it" (Matt 16:18-19). Those two old, Lutheran pastors are gone now. But there remains a line of thinking I want to develop.

If we understand that Jesus Christ is the One in whom, through whom, the kingdom of heaven has arrived, and thus the One in whom, through whom, heaven and earth are reunited, then what he says next to Peter has profound implications. "I will give you the keys of the kingdom of heaven, and whatever you bind on earth will be bound in heaven, and whatever you loose on earth will be loosed in heaven" (Matt 16:19). Essentially, the church of Peter is commissioned with participating in this reconciliation of heaven and earth. It is called to embody God's kingdom of self-giving, reconciling love and mercy to a world estranged from it. But there lurks a temptation within such a commission. Behind every commission looms the threat of self-inflation.

In other words, it is a natural assumption that Peter is worthy of the calling. And if he is worthy of the calling, then there must be something intrinsic to Peter—some type of competence—that marks him as such. Certainly Jesus Christ—like all good leaders in our world vested with hierarchical authority—wouldn't commission incompetence! Clearly Jesus Christ is *lifting-up* Peter's *rock-like* qualities, yes? In return, certainly Peter's *rock-like* leadership will assist in *lifting-up* Jesus Christ's authority? Yes. Peter will certainly be implicated in Jesus' *lifting-up*. But in a way Peter can't begin to fathom at the time.

In conferring the keys of the kingdom upon Peter, let me ask: is Jesus Christ reinforcing the world's sense of competence—now in the form of *church*—by decorating it with his name? Or is such a move how Jesus Christ will demonstrate the gratuitous nature of his *commitment* to his church, a commitment so profound that even the church's competence for conducting his ministry is revealed to be a divine gift?

"Pastor," declared the voice on the other end, "Jack Anderson died." The voice continued, "I understand that he is a member of your congregation." Before I had time to respond, to indicate that I have never heard of this individual in my life, the funeral director added, "The family is here with me and we want to know whether Thursday or Friday morning works best for you."

"Jack who?" I quickly responded. Nobody in the congregation by the name Jack had been sick or actively dying. And no deaths had been brought to my attention.

"Jack Anderson," repeated the funeral director. "The family here with me indicated that the church you serve was his church."

"Just a moment," I responded. I covered the phone with my hand and looked over to my secretary and asked, "Hey, Sally did you know a Jack Anderson?"

Sally quickly piped up—she'd served as the congregational secretary for over 25 years—and declared, "Oh yes, I remember Jack. He hasn't worshiped here in twenty-plus years. He was upset about something and left. We haven't heard from him since."

"Well," I responded, "Jack died."

Sally shot back with a smile, "I'm guessing the family wants you to do his funeral because 'this was his church.'" She added, "He walked away. But this was still *his* church." She knew the drill.

"Yep."

I got back on the phone with the funeral director. "Ok, I'm back. Sorry about that." I continued, "Yes, looking at my schedule for this week, Friday morning works. Normally we schedule morning funerals for 10:00 a.m."

"That'll work," replied the funeral director.

"Now," I followed up, "when the family is done meeting with you, I need you to send them over to the church so that we can plan the worship service, determine the hymns, Bible readings, the type of luncheon they desire, and so on." But behind all the funeral details, the real goal of the meeting in this case was discovery. I had no idea who this man was. Although the subject of a funeral sermon is the Word of God, as a funeral sermon is not a eulogy, it's good to have a personality, a life, to provide a framework in which to proclaim the Gospel.

"I sure will, pastor."

"And if you have any questions between now and the day of the funeral, just call," I added.

How many times this type of situation has occurred in the congregations I have served I can't count. Of the scores of funerals I have officiated, I'm guessing that ten percent of them have involved a deceased person who claimed in life to belong to a church—the one I was then serving—whose threshold had rarely been crossed.

+ + + + + + +

Briefly, a word on members and memberships...

When studies indicate that mainline Christianity in the United States is diminishing, that our denomination is declining precipitously per membership numbers, I remember the key term: *membership*. *Membership* is not synonymous with *discipleship*. Both—members and disciples—are sustained by the grace of Jesus Christ. The latter are animated by that grace more frequently.

At no point in the Gospel narratives do I find Jesus Christ seeking *members*. As if the Christian church operated by a model similar to a local fraternal organization. I joined one years ago because my son was playing for a sports team sponsored by them. Though I went through an initiation rite, I have not been in active fellowship with them for years. But my membership card still affords me the benefits of being considered a member. As long as I pay my dues. Activity, though a good thing, is not a prerequisite for maintaining *membership*. Such is the case, from my experience, with regard to how Christians often relate to *their* congregations. It's a *membership* model.

But Jesus Christ calls us into a *discipleship* model through which we are called to his ministry of reconciliation (II Cor 5:18ff.), to be daily "transformed by the renewing of our minds," and thus no longer remaining as ones who are "conformed to this world" (Rom 12:2). A discipleship model creates an atmosphere of commitment and transformation, of spiritual growth and an ever-deepening sense of the love of God revealed in Jesus Christ. On the other hand, a membership model often gravitates toward the lowest common denominator. Perhaps one is considered a voting member (at annual meetings) if they have given of their wealth (something, anything!) and/or communed once during the prior calendar year.

A discipleship model is informed by a Baptism which is expressed in the daily attempt to live the Lordship of Jesus Christ in thought, word, and deed. A membership model reduces Baptism to an insurance policy which I can take out and then forget. Have children. Then repeat.

Connected to this subject, I want to reframe the matter of *open* and *closed* Communion within the framework of *discipleship* (as opposed to *membership*). When the matter is posed within the framework of discipleship, Communion is neither *open* nor *closed*. It becomes, on the one hand, the Means of Grace by which Christ's disciples are restored to his lordship, nourished to conduct his ministry of love and mercy among themselves and to the world. On the other hand, Communion becomes an expression of Christ's radical hospitality and abundance to the community. Again, within the framework of *discipleship*—not membership—Communion is neither *open* nor *closed*. It becomes a feast of faith's nourishment and empowerment for the sake of conducting Christ's ministry, and a witness to Christ's hospitality and abundant love to the visitor. The body of Christ is called to a *ministry of reconciliation*. It not a ministry of institutional affiliation.

Such a framing of the matter of *open* and *closed* communion is conducted from the perspective that *discipleship* is expressive of the promise that knowledge of Jesus Christ is relational, participatory, transformational knowledge. And let us note well: the convenience alligator which the membership model feeds has an insatiable appetite. That alligator always turns on its handlers.

+ + + + + + +

Back to Jack Anderson: as we planned for his funeral our congregation cut no corners. We worshiped, proclaimed, and demonstrated to Jack's family and friends the God who loved him into existence and redeemed him through that same love. No doubt folks will complain that the sermon sounded like it was spoken by a pastor who "didn't know Jack."

The intensity of that text study remains memorable. And those words from the Bible passage were repeated several times: ". . . and the gates of Hades will not prevail against it" (Matt 16:18b). The words have spawned a question. Namely: could it be that we become so enamored with harnessing ourselves to the authority we *assume* Peter *should* have that we overlook Peter's shortcomings and how those shortcomings are exploited for the sake of revealing the depth of God's commitment and mercy?

The *rock* (Peter)—only four short verses later—does what rocks do best: he becomes a stumbling block. "Get behind me, Satan! You are a stumbling block to me; for you are setting your mind not on divine things but on human things" (Matt 16:23). In response to Jesus' declaration that he "must go to Jerusalem and undergo great suffering at the hands of the elders and chief priests and scribes, and be killed, and on the third day be raised" (Matt 16:21), that, essentially, his authority will be demonstrated in vulnerability and self-giving love to a people who reject him, we learn that Peter will tolerate nothing of the sort. Peter's working concept of authority is a *strong-arm* one.

Let us observe Peter: feel threatened? Cut off an ear (John 18:10). Fear being identified with a particular Lord who goes by *Jesus of Nazareth*? Self-preservation's prescription is easy: Deny, deny, deny (Matt 26:69–75). And let us not forget the "walking on water" episode (See Matt 14:28ff.). Peter's use of *me* has always been troubling. That is, upon seeing Jesus Christ walking on the wind-battered waters, he called out, "Lord if it is you command *me* to come to you on the water." (Matt 14:28) The impulse to self-preservation has a way of forcing us to forget those who are with us in our wave-battered boats. Our instincts to self-preservation have a way of magnifying our self-centeredness. It is interesting how such a fundamental theme often gets missed in this episode.

Peter is a reminder that rocks sink. Peter is a reminder that rocks can be dull. Peter is a reminder that if rocks aren't making the path bumpy, then they're blocking the way altogether. Rocks block entrances. Let us relish the irony: Jesus Christ reveals that he is "the Way, the Truth, and the Life" (John 14:6). And then the Way commissions the *rock* as his chief disciple. Peter is a reminder that rocks have a tendency of getting in the way of, working at cross-purposes to, the Way who has called them.

In our bondage to Peter's strong-arm thinking *Petros* becomes a foundation on which to construct an ecclesial edifice befitting our hierarchies and their thirst for centralization and purity specs. Yet crucified with Christ and raised with him, such a foundation—*Petros*—becomes a servant of its Lord for the world.

A looming lunch together at the local Chinese buffet kept the conversation on Matthew 16:18 cordial and collegial. Again, the verse at the center of the discussion: *"And I tell you, you are Peter [Petros], and this rock [petra] I will build my church, and the gates of Hades will not prevail against it."* Permit me to offer a brief rehash of the arguments:

The old pastor to my right declared that Peter, *Petros*, is the *rock* upon which the church is founded by Jesus Christ. Indeed, he asserted, it is good for the One, Holy, Catholic, and *Apostolic* Church to trace its leadership lineage back to Peter. The Historic Episcopate, he pointed out, was important for the visible unity and authority of the church's witness.

And the second old pastor cleared his throat with a sharp, yet cordial, rebuttal: no, the *rock* upon which Christ has founded his church is the *petra*, the confession of Jesus Christ as Lord. It is a confession which expresses itself in the proper administration of Word and Sacrament conducted from and for the confession of the Word of God. One asserted *Petros*. And the other declared *petra*. In retrospect they were both right. *And* wrong.

Petros is a reflection of us. We are rocks called by The Way to conduct his ministry. Rocks who quickly become stumbling blocks. Rocks who can be dull, obtuse, with regard to perceiving the nature and presence of Christ's kingdom. Rocks who can bruise and hurt. Rocks who have a habit of blocking access to the very Way they are called to reveal. Rocks who can't seem to imagine that a foundation in Christ is resurrected from such things as wounds, vulnerability, and—ultimately—death. To say nothing of repentance and humility. Rocks who have a difficult time featuring themselves as *ungodly* apart from God's unilateral work of redemption on their behalf (see Rom 5:1-11). Rocks who waver between the call to live from the promise of God's abundant life (John 17:3), and the default drive for self-preservation (which becomes the engine which drives *strong-arm* authority). *Petros* is an instrument of Christ's mercy one moment, and a conduit of the devil's retribution in the next.

Petra is a confession which soon betrays the confessor's ignorance regarding the nature and scope of the Lordship to which obedience is declared. *Petra* is a wavering declaration of allegiance which is soon crucified on the truth that one cannot serve two masters (Matt 6:24). *Petra* is a positive response to Christ's bid to follow him though one has kept an eye open for more appealing bids. *Petra* is a confession of fidelity to a kingdom of divine vulnerability and joy made by a heart encased in anxiety, fear, and resentment.

Petras and *petra*. To exchange the former with the latter is to replace a lineage-based authority for one normally grounded in *right thinking* or *right doing* (theology, liturgy, social justice stance, *et. al.*). Both perennially succumb to the temptation to derive identity—to justify ourselves—apart from Christ's sustaining faithfulness and mercy. Both establish corresponding hierarchies with a symptomatic atmosphere of Peter-like authority (perhaps veiled by a veneer *grace* and *welcome*). Both become pharisaic orthodoxies hell-bent—in the process of witnessing the kingdom of heaven—on protecting the purity of their respective authorities.

"And I tell you, you are Peter [Petros], and this rock [petra] I will build my church . . ." Given what we know about the whole story, the role these *rocks* play in the Gospel story, perhaps we may finally see the obverse side of Jesus Christ's commitment to his church is his good humor and forbearance regarding the *rocks* he has called to demonstrate the Way. So bent on cultivating and maintaining the purity of our authority, we have missed the humor, the grace-filled teasing, dispensed by Jesus Christ in the genre of observational comedy, *about us, the church*. Humor and its close cousin humility are often the first casualties when authority is threatened.

". . . *and the gates of Hades will not prevail against it.*" Such is the promise the church fails to hear when it is preoccupied with securing and consolidating itself in the image of the world's *strong-arm* concept of authority. That Hades will not prevail against the church is God's promise that through us, yet despite us, the kingdom of Heaven will flourish. It is the promise that the rocks who have been called to conduct Christ's ministry are indeed—by means of the Holy Spirit—*good soil* for such an enterprise.

To hear the promise of this God requires first being crucified to our longing for authority on the world's terms. From such a crucifixion is resurrected the confession that the church's authority to conduct the task for which it has been *called out* (*ecclesia*) is extrinsic to its sin-bound abilities. Our rocky hearts are made fertile by this promise.

Sarah laughed when she considered the discrepancy between the barrenness of her reproductive organs and God's promise of a child. Isaac was a child of that laughter, a witness to the promise of commitment, of life, stirring within such barrenness. Perhaps the day will come when such laughter burbles up from our collective, churchly bellies. Maybe such an opportunity for laughter will one day be inscribed into our official liturgies, promoted in our theological curricula.

It is the laughter of those who understand their competence and authority comes from beyond themselves in the unceasing grace of God. Perhaps such a laughter will translate into a collective sense of humor, and thus sense of humility, which understands true authority to be kenotic, or an expression of the crucified Christ who has called us (see Phil 2:5–11). In such cruciformity is resurrected a gaze which begins to see the crucifixions of this world as the locations from which—and in which—we are called to minister.

In the church's response to that call is its clearest, most visible expression of authority, its most profound hallelujah.

Conclusion: Broken Hallelujahs

There's a blaze of light in every word;
it doesn't matter which you heard,
the holy, or the broken Hallelujah!

—Leonard Cohen, "Hallelujah" (verse 3)[1]

My image is the last thing I expected to see in a cemetery. My name appears on my mother's tombstone. But that, I suppose you might say, is "par for the course." The names of children appear on the tombstones of parents all over the world. This is not my name, but my *image*. And it isn't a family member's tombstone. Or mine.

My image appears on a black marble slab which covers a burial plot. It is one among several pictures, chronologically ordered from the head of the marble slab to the foot. The pictures trace various stages of a life.

---

1. Alan Light remarks on this verse—especially with reference to "a blaze of light in every word"—and I couldn't agree more, "Every word, holy or broken—this the fulcrum of the song as Cohen first wrote it. Like our forefathers, and the Bible heroes who formed the foundation of Western ethics and principles, we will be hurt, tested, and challenged. Love will break our hearts, music will offer solace that we may or may not hear, we will be faced with joy and with pain. But Cohen is telling us, without resorting to sentimentality, not to surrender to despair or nihilism. Critics may have fixated on the gloom and doom of his lyrics, but this is his offering of hope and perseverance in the face of a cruel world. Holy or broken, there is still hallelujah." (Light, *The Holy or the Broken*, 24)

In that picture I'm vested. I'm engaged in the act of baptizing a baby boy. I'll call him Nolan. His mother is cradling his little body. She is holding his little head over the baptismal font. My right hand is dowsing his head with water. I remember the day. I remember the moment. I remember the beams of joy which radiated from the faces of the parents and grandparents. I remember the photos which were snapped following the worship service. I remember speaking the words:

I baptize you in the name of the Father, and of the Son, and of the Holy Spirit.

I visited his grave many times since his death. But his tombstone and its marble slab had not yet been installed. Now I understood why it took so much time. The writing, designs, and pictures are extensive. Before the installation of his tombstone and marble slab his grave had been marked by a metal spike which bore a name/date placard.

Marble intensifies a sense of finality. The period of the provisional had passed. He is dead. It was true. I shuddered again. It was as if I had received word of his death for the first time. That smile, that energy, that personality . . . where did it go? The picture of me baptizing baby Nolan conjures the joy of that day. Standing over his grave, I was suspended between a joyous memory and a horrifying reality. It is a reality I still struggle to believe. I had baptized dozens of children. This was one was lying in a grave. This one severely tested my *baptismal faith.*

> Do you not know that all of us who have been baptized into Christ Jesus were baptized into his death? Therefore we have been buried with him by baptism into death, so that, just as Christ was raised from the dead by the glory of the Father, so we too might walk in newness of life. For if we have been united with him in a death like his, we will certainly be united with him in a resurrection like his. (Rom 6: 3–5)

Baptism has always ignited a struggle in me between two regimes, that of creation and that of new creation; that of death and that of life; that of accusation and that of grace.

I didn't want to be there. Any other place in the entire world would have sufficed. I dreaded this moment from the minute I received word of the death. The parents' grief was unimaginable. Nolan, some months (I don't remember how many) past three, had died in an accident that could have happened to any child. To any parents. As a parent myself the *any* is a truth I know deep in my bones.

CONCLUSION: BROKEN HALLELUJAHS

But I couldn't *not* be there. Though my heart had been broken open for this family, I was called to be there. The living God had equipped me to be there. We suffer the gifts of God. Perhaps that is the definition of vocation: *suffering the gifts, and thus calling, of God in the place where God has called us*. And *there* is by the open casket of a of a three-year-old boy just minutes before the funeral service was to begin. *There* is that location where a pastor must hold it together. The weeping will come later.

Amid a sanctuary packed to overflow, a pocket of suspended time had been created at this casket which was soon to be closed. Nolan's parents had been escorted over by the funeral director for the final goodbye. They would gaze upon their child for the final time. In the mother's arms was their one-year-old son. He was holding a couple of Matchbox cars. In retrospect, those Matchbox cars were sacramental. They bore the promise of life.

Lying in that small, open casket—I forget its external color and its interior fabric—was a little boy with wavy locks piled above his forehead. It was a crown of youthful beauty. The embalming made him appear as a cherub in repose. He appeared as boy resting between play sessions, about to waken at any moment. He wore white tennis shoes, a pair of khakis, and a short-sleeved, collared orange shirt with three buttons. Only one was buttoned. Nolan's little right hand rested on his little left hand. They were placed on his waist. I studied those hands. I shook that little right hand many times in the post-worship receiving line. I could still feel his grip. As we stood there—parents and little brother, grandparents, aunts and uncles, pastor—the sanctuary and its people seemed to disappear.

Each family member, in their own way, through their own liturgy of love, said goodbye. And then Nolan's mother lowered his little brother to the side of the casket. It was a vantage point from which he could see and touch his big brother. Suddenly, naturally, amid this liturgy of grief, emerged a liturgy of play. In words coherent only to a boy of one, perhaps which only his older brother was ever able to comprehend, his little brother spoke. He then offered one of his two Matchbox cars to his older brother.

Because death does not accept such offers, his little brother gently placed it above Nolan's hands, on his stomach. I'm assuming the reasoning was that he would find it there when nap time was over. Nolan was always ready to play after naps.

And his little brother continued to speak to his older brother. From his mouth also emanated the sounds of a revving engine. He drove his other little Matchbox car down an imaginary, winding road in the space over his brother. They were the sounds of play. And, were playtime to last long enough, perhaps such sounds and chatter would lure his older brother from rest. And Nolan would arise to the vitality a little brother knows. Naturally, of course. That is what his little brother knew: older brothers rise to play. They never turn down the opportunity. Older brothers are reliable that way. Certainly, this was an unrequited offer of play by a child too young to comprehend his environment.

But this was also a liturgy. Not a liturgy planned and conducted by a trained church leader. It was the intuitive liturgy of vitality and wholeness conducted by a small child. It was an instinctive, natural invitation to play. In the moments prior to Nolan's funeral his little brother demonstrated that resurrection should be expected. Older brothers rise. That is what they do. The glorious promise of new creation had—briefly—become a natural expectation.

I have stood over that tombstone and marble slab many, many times. Too many to count. As long as the etched images on the marble slab remain, Nolan and I are bound together at the scene of his Baptism. At the scene of his burial. Bound together at two locations of death. And promise.

Each time I stand over his tombstone and marble slab, my mind's eye pierces the marble, the concrete, the metal . . . and there finds a waxen cherub, his little right hand gently resting upon his left. Time has stood still according to this vision. He still radiates the pregnant pause of a little boy between play periods, the interim nap. And each time I stand over his tombstone, his marble slab, I see a Matchbox car resting on a little orange shirt just above his layered hands.

When so many offered for his funeral service flowers to express sorrow over death, Nolan's little brother offered up the gift of play. With that Matchbox car was a little brother's offer to play. It was a *call to play*. One to which older brothers naturally respond. Just as the people of God naturally respond to the *call to worship*. Within that grave rests both a young child and a little brother's Matchbox car. The latter is a sign of what awaits.

It is tempting to associate the beauty of the church's hallelujahs with the magnificent, calculated liturgies of our worship spaces. Yet that grave is a reminder that our most profound hallelujahs arise from the depths of our pain, our grief. Our deaths. "The love of God does not find, but creates, that which is pleasing to it,"[2] asserted Martin Luther. Such hallelujahs, bearing the concealed promise of new creation, draw our gaze to the deep,

2. LW 31:53

intimate manner of God's creativity, to the brokenness which has become the womb of God's life-creating agency revealed in the crucified and risen One. They emanate from the broken sighs uttered from both ends of the church's ministry, from laity and pastors alike. They draw our attention to the faithfulness of the One who stirs within, who wells up from the depths, with the promise to make us whole.

Big brothers arise from naps to play with little brothers. That is what they were created to do. The promise of new creation, its vitality and wholeness, was preached before the service ever started. In the play taking place over that casket.

+ + + + + + +

"God's call and Christ's cross," wrote the late Alan E. Lewis, "are not only mutually conditioned: they are the same reality. God calls humanity and the church through the crucified and risen Son; and there is no vocation that is not Christologically determined."[3] Within the context of such Christ-logic Lewis asserted that "Ministry is theology's polygraph, its infallible lie-detecting test, revealing the truth of what the church believes and the identity of whom she worships—the God of the cross or the false deities of her cultural ideology."[4] If this is the case, and my experience corroborates such a confession, pastoral ministry is a ministry which ministers from the cross of Christ to the crosses of Christ. It is a ministry which, inhabiting the gaze of the crucified God, not only "look[s] only into the depths,"[5] but serves among, within them. Created by crucifixion, it is seeing which ignites solidarity's serving, its ministry.

Pastoral ministry—one called by, derived from, the crucified and risen One—is a ministry immersed in context, its rawness and coarseness. It demonstrates a love which transgresses established hierarchies and boundaries. It can be messy and awkward. It is emptied of self-serving authority. Aware of one's own crucifixions, it is free to see and serve the crucifixions of others. Aware of the depth of one's sin—ever mindful of one's brokenness and capability for darkness—the minister can be a fountain of grace and mercy among and to fellow sinners.

---

3. Lewis, "*Vocation* in the Ecclesia Crucis," 113.
4. Ibid.
5. LW 21:299. See also Anthony, *Promising Nothing*, 151.

The ultimate beauty of such a ministry lies in its broken hallelujahs. The beauty of the church's hallelujahs are not the heights to which they ascend, but the shattered, crucified depths from which they are voiced. In those depths is the liturgy—its spectrum of expressions—of Christ's hallelujah.

Bibliography

Anthony, Neal J. *Cross Narratives: Martin Luther's Christology and the Location of Redemption*. Princeton Theological Monograph Series. With a foreword by Vitor Westhelle. Eugene, OR: Pickwick, 2010.

———. *Promising Nothing: Christology Suspended from the Cross*. Eugene, OR: Pickwick, 2021.

"Epitome." In *The Book of Concord: The Confessions of the Evangelical Lutheran Church*. Edited by Robert Kolb and Timothy J. Wengert, translated by Charles Arand, 486 – 523. Minneapolis: Fortress, 2000.

Jeremias, Joachim. *Jerusalem in the Time of Jesus*. Philadelphia: Fortress, 1969.

Lewis, Alan E. "*Unmasking Idolatries: Vocation in the* Ecclesia Crucis." In *Incarnational Ministry: The Presence of Christ in Church, Society, and Family*. With a foreword by David Alan Hubbard. Edited by Christian D. Kettler and Todd H. Speidell, 110-128. Colorado Springs: Helmers & Howard, 1990.

Light, Alan. *The Holy or the Broken: Leonard Cohen, Jeff Buckley and the Unlikely Ascent of "Hallelujah."* New York: Atria, 2012.

Luther, Martin. *Works*. (Cited LW) Edited by Jaroslav Pelikan et al. 75 vols. St. Louis: Concordia, 1955-76.

———. "The Large Catechism." In *The Book of Concord: The Confessions of the Evangelical Lutheran Church*. Edited by Robert Kolb and Timothy J. Wengert, translated by Charles Arand, 377-480. Minneapolis: Fortress, 2000.

———. "The Small Catechism." In *The Book of Concord: The Confessions of the Evangelical Lutheran Church*. Edited by Robert Kolb and Timothy J. Wengert, translated by Charles Arand, 345-375. Minneapolis: Fortress, 2000.

Lyotard, Jean-Francois. *The Postmodern Condition: A Report on Knowledge*. Translated from the French by Geoff Bennington and Brian Massumi, foreword by Fredric Jameson. Minneapolis: University of Minnesota Press, 1984.

Zscheile, Dwight. "Will the ELCA be Gone in 30 Years?" Faith+Lead, Sept. 5, 2019. Accessed Sept. 23, 2023. https://faithlead.org/blog/decline/.

Subject Index

Alcohol (and academia), 90–91
Anselm of Canterbury, 41

Baptism, 11, 62–64, 82, 116
Barth, Karl, 84

Calvin, John, 84
Campbell, Joseph, 84
"Casket Crawlers," 32, 37–38
"Casket packing," 35
Church (see also Ministry)
    and authority (the nature of), 103–114
    and biblical interpretation, 102–114
    and "blue" and "red" Christians, 95, 99
    and Communion practice (*open* and *closed*), 110
    as expression of crucified Christ (cruciform existence), 113–14
    and Historic Episcopate, 103, 112
    and humor (in the function of biblical interpretation), 103, 105–7, 113
    and humor (as related to Christian self-awareness and humility), 113–14
    and justification, 112–13
    "marks" of, xv
    and membership/attendance decline, 104
    and membership versus discipleship, 109–110
    and Peter (see Church and authority)
    and visible unity, 103–114
    as vocation (see also Ministry and vocation), xv
    without high heels and make-up, xi–xiii
Cohen, Leonard, xv–xvi, 115
Crucified God, 70

Dehumanization (see Racism), 95–96
Deus ex machina, 70

Ecclesiology, xv, 102–114

Fall (The), 89

Gifts (of God), 21–22

Hallelujah (Leonard Cohen song), xv, 115

Imago Dei (see also Ministry and *Imago Dei*), xviii, 31, 46–47, 59, 89
    and *Abusus non tollit*, 11

Jeremias, Joachim, 49
Justice (see Ministry and social justice; Ministry and Christ-Justice)

Lewis, Alan E., 119
Light, Alan, xv, 115
Luther, Martin, xv, 11, 38, 118
Lyotard, Jean-Francois, 95

SUBJECT INDEX

Magical thinking, 78–79
Metanarratives, 95–97
Ministry
    and anxiety/depression
        (experiencing), 84–87
    and atonement theory, 41–47
    and candidate (pastor) call process,
        48–54
    and chaplaincy, 4–6, 26–28
    and Christ-justice, 58–59
    and death of infants/children, 60–67,
        115–18
    and domestic crisis response, 1–12
    and dying and death, 22–31, 74–82,
        115–18
    and empathetic understanding (the
        development of), 72–73, 92
    and evil, 58
    and funeral preaching, 40–41, 44–45
    and funeral viewing (the decision to
        conduct), 79–80
    and funeral visitation, 32–38
    and grief (ministering while
        grieving), 61–62, 64–65, 67,
        68–82
    and home visitation, 13–15
    and *Imago Dei* (seeking of), xviii, 51
    and ministering to addiction, 15–21,
        34, 45–46
    as ministry of reconciliation, xii – xiv
    and "pastoral pause," 7–8
    and politics, 93–101
    and preaching, 39–47
    and priesthood of all believers, 82
    and purity (identity derived from
        category of), 49–53
    and relationships (within the
        congregation), 74–82
    and self-awareness, 91
    and self-care, 82–92
    and self-medicating, 87–92
    and sexual boundaries, 48–59
    and social (retributive) justice, 57–59
    and theologian of the cross (the
        making of), 68–73
    Under the Cross (Cruciform), 102–
        114, 119
    and visible righteousness, 57–59
    and vocation, 66–67
    and wisdom (as perspective of faith),
        71

Parable of the Good Samaritan, 48–51
Parable of the Barren Fig Tree, 39–40, 46
Piety, 71
Postmodernity (see also Metanarratives),
    95
Promise (see Word of God)

Racism (see also dehumanization)
    as covert racism, 95–96
    as overt racism, 95–96
Resurrection (Promise), 12, 55
    as liturgy, 117–18
    and purification of, 53, 59

Tillich, Paul, 84
Time of Trump, 93–101

Word of God, 31, 81, 101
    as lens for seeing others, 38

Zero-sum thinking, 97

Scripture Index

Genesis

1:26	40
18:13ff.	105

Exodus

34:7	21

Numbers

19:10b-13	49–50

Matthew

6:24	112
14: 28	111
14:28ff.	111
16:18	102, 111
16:18b	110
16:18–19	107
16:19	107
16:21	111
16:23	111
18:21	40
26:69–75	111

Luke

10:25–37	48
13: 6–9	39
13:8	39
23:34	40

John

1:5	92
1:14	xviii
14:6	111
17:3	112
18:10	111

Romans

3:21	43, 50
5: 1–11	112
6:3–5	116
12:2	109

2 Corinthians

5:18	xii, xiii
5:18ff.	109

Galatians

3:22–23	40
6:15	101

Philippians

2: 5–11	113

Colossians

1:26	43

www.ingramcontent.com/pod-product-compliance
Lightning Source LLC
Chambersburg PA
CBHW071214160426
43196CB00012B/2303

"*Broken Hallelujahs* is a profound and gripping articulation of Christian pastoral leadership that relentlessly pursues Christ's merciful grace in recognizing the image of God in each person. With ruthless honesty and through stunning stories, Rev. Dr. Anthony unmasks the pretenses and distortions that conceal the liberating power of the crucified and risen Christ. This work is eminently saturated with healthy insights of spiritual care. Read, digest, and relish this gift!"

—**David deFreese**, Former Bishop, Nebraska Synod, ELCA

"In a world like ours, brokenness lurks within everything that's beautiful. But since it's a God-created world, in everything that's broken, something beautiful can be revealed. With riveting and raw storytelling, Neal Anthony traces the hand of God's love amidst psychic pain, alcoholic rages, tribalistic identitarianism, prairie tedium, dissolute lust, and, frankly, the manure of ministry."

—**John A. Nunes**, President, California Lutheran University

"In *Broken Hallelujahs*, Neal Anthony candidly and vulnerably reveals the soul of pastoral ministry. Through anecdotes that are by turn poignant and humorous, sublime and ridiculous, he invites the reader to discover the depth of a life surrendered to the call to serve. With deep feeling and intellectual heft, Anthony makes these pages a portal not only into the breadth and depth of the pastor's vocation, but into any believer's—or seeker's—exploration of what it means to live as a person of faith."

—**Brian Maas**, Bishop Emeritus, Nebraska Synod, ELCA

"In his honest recollections, Pastor Neal Anthony reveals a truth of our calling to the ministry of Word and Sacrament: God's people are always an absurd mixture of holiness and carnality, capable of exquisite beauty one minute and horrific trauma the next. Pr. Anthony's deep love for the church is apparent—that same love shapes this memoir, which is at turns painful, authentic, troubling, and delightful."

—**Scott Alan Johnson**, Bishop, Nebraska Synod, ELCA